# The New
# Dr. Cookie Cookbook

# The New
# Dr. Cookie Cookbook

### Dessert Your Way to Health with More Than 150 Delicious Low-fat Cookies, Cakes, and Treats

~~~

**Marvin A. Wayne, M.D.**
**Stephen R. Yarnall, M.D.**

Quill
New York

It is the policy of William Morrow and Company, Inc., and its imprints and affiliates, recognizing the importance of preserving what has been written, to print the books we publish on acid-free paper, and we exert our best efforts to that end.

Library of Congress Cataloging-in-Publication Data

Wayne, Marvin A., 1943–
    The new Dr. Cookie cookbook / Marvin A. Wayne,
  Stephen R. Yarnall.
        p.        cm.
    Includes bibliographical references and index.
    ISBN 0-688-12222-1
    1. Desserts.   2. Low-fat diet—Recipes.   3. Low-calorie diet—
  Recipes.   I. Yarnall, Stephen R.   II. Title.
  TX773.W36   1994
  641.86'—dc20                                              93–2501
                                                              CIP

Printed in the United States of America

First Quill Edition

1   2   3   4   5   6   7   8   9   10

BOOK DESIGN BY RICHARD ORIOLO

To our families,
whose encouragement and support
helped make this dream possible!

# Preface

ood is terribly important to me. It means communication with my family and with other cultures, it means joy and comfort, it means fulfillment and sharing. I have always seen food in this light.

In 1982 my time with rheumatic fever as a child finally caught up with me and they replaced my floppy aortic valve with an artificial valve. No, my bad valve was not due to bad eating habits but rather to the disease of my childhood. When I woke up in the recovery room I had one big party . . . one great celebration of joy . . . all in my mind. Then it hit me! Dr. Lester Sauvage had saved my life and four dieticians were trying to kill me!

The diet offered me, me being the food lover, was typical of the thinking of the time. No fat, no salt, no color, no flavor, no variety, no wine . . . it was just great. Blah. Since that time we have managed to calm the food right-wingers who always seem to go to the extreme. I am thankful.

The authors of this joyfully titled cookbook, Drs. Wayne and Yarnall, are urging all of us to avoid the extremes. The middle road seems to be best in terms of diet. Cut down on fat and salt because we have used too much in the past. But to totally avoid same is to put up with bland food that usually results in poor eating habits and certainly a lack of joy at the table. There is, in my mind, no point in a diet that bores you to death. Better to die of joy!

I will admit that these two doctors have given this book a subtitle that almost sounds like a gag line: *Dessert Your Way to Health with More Than 150 Delicious Low-fat Cookies, Cakes, and Treats.* It sounds too good to be true, but then the title is really a light exaggeration. The authors swing to the other side as they oppose the current "Stop Enjoying Your Food" movement.

They suggest a middle of the road approach to eating, and certainly to lifestyles. No single diet is right for everyone. Yarnall even told me that I could enjoy my beloved pork spareribs now and then, but then he added, "but not too often. It all depends on your lifestyle and your ability to deal with fats and salts. Everyone is different. It all depends."

Hey, I like this guy. And I like his approach to cooking. Please do not think that this book is offering only desserts. Rather, it offers a very sensible approach to eating in our time, a time in which everyone claims that they are eating a much healthier diet—but a time in which the chocolate chip cookie stands, the chocolate bar companies, and the fancy extra rich ice cream manufacturers are doing a booming business. Like never before!

Take heart and use these recipes to placate your foodie guilt and just cut down a bit. "It all depends." Aside from great recipes, you will find a gold mine of healthy information about a decent, delicious, and sensible diet. Like I said, I like these guys.

—JEFF SMITH
The Frugal Gourmet

# Foreword

**W**ithout food we cannot live, yet the wrong kinds of foods can shorten our lives. The breaking of bread is also a time when we come together and share. To a large degree, we meet and eat and form our futures in more ways than one.

As a cardiovascular surgeon and research director, I appreciate the value of keeping people from becoming heart patients. While surgery can relieve symptoms and extend life, preventing the development of heart disease in the first place is far better.

Drs. Yarnall and Wayne have done all of us a favor by writing this book and adding to the joy of eating, while at the same time helping us stay healthy. They have shown us that a good diet can be tasty and fun. Life should be a joy and this book is an aid to making it so.

—LESTER R. SAUVAGE, M.D.
*founder and medical director,*
*The Hope Heart Institute*

# Acknowledgments

Any book is a labor of love and *The New Dr. Cookie Cookbook* is the product of the love and labor of many individuals–too many to acknowledge fully.

Our primary acknowledgment is of Joan Wayne–for her genius in the kitchen and organizational skills at the word processor. Also, the Wayne children, Michelle and Dana, have contributed to proofreading, typing, and tasting!

The book was originally encouraged by Bill Adler, our agent, and seen to completion by Will Schwalbe of William Morrow. Thanks to Carole Berglie for expert copyediting.

Many thanks are due to: Anthony Loew, for his cover photograph; Michael Weiss, for the luscious food photographs; Roscoe Betsill, who styled the food so brilliantly; and Randi Barritt for her skill in finding props. And also to Mary DeVlieger-Johnson for all her help during the shoot.

Huge thanks are due to Mary Goodbody for her astute comments and all her help in preparing the manuscript for publication. And to LeeAnna Nicholson, for coordinating typing efforts on early drafts.

And we are profoundly grateful to Lester R. Sauvage, M.D., for his foreword and the incomparable Jeff Smith for providing a preface.

We thank our many friends for their taste-testing and encouragement. We particularly thank Lynn O'Malley and her carbo-loading running associates, who have encouraged us in this work while pursuing ultra-marathon training and competition! (They run more to eat more!)

Special thanks, too, to dietician Nancy Miller for her review of the manuscript and helpful comments.

Finally, we thank you for reading this book and discovering with us that you can indeed have your cake . . . and cookies, too.

# Contents

Preface
by Jeff Smith, The Frugal Gourmet
vii

Foreword
by Lester R. Sauvage, M.D.
ix

Acknowledgments
xi

Introduction
1

Chapter 1
**Cookies**
15

Chapter 2
**Cakes**
59

Chapter 3
**Pies and Tarts**
83

Chapter 4
**Fruit Desserts**
97

Chapter 5
## Muffins and Biscuits
115

Chapter 6
## Quick Breads
143

Chapter 7
## Yeast Breads
175

Index
219

Contents

# Introduction

Go ahead. Eat dessert. Please.

We're doctors, both highly trained medical professionals who believe wholeheartedly in a healthful lifestyle that includes eating the right foods. We believe that good nutrition is directly linked to good health, and we practice what we preach by eating diets rich in fiber and complex carbohydrates and low in fat. We eat very little red meat. We do eat lots of fruits and vegetables, grains, and legumes. We eat low-fat dairy products in moderation. What's more, we exercise faithfully (some say fanatically!) and encourage our patients to do so, too, within the confines of their particular health restrictions.

Why are we writing a book with more than 160 recipes for desserts and breads? Does that make sense? After all, desserts are sinfully fattening, appealing to all the worst instincts of humankind: excess, indulgence, greed, sloth. . . . Wrong. Desserts are the best part of many meals. They make you feel good because they satisfy the appetite as no raw vegetable salad, rice pilaf, or pasta extravaganza can. They are sweet and filling, often warm and comforting. They're fun and celebratory. As firmly as we believe in eating right and exercising regularly, we believe in enjoying life to the fullest. And for us, that means eating desserts and home-baked breads.

This does not mean just *any* dessert. We recommend desserts that are intentionally low in fat and calories. This can be as simple as a bowl of ripe strawberries or as extravagant as our Chocolate Decadence with Raspberry Sauce (page 76). We have dedicated a good portion of the last several years to creating desserts, muffins, biscuits, and breads that defy tradition by tasting good while being remarkably low-fat and low-calorie. With our recipes you won't miss out on flavor, but your waistline will thank you. Further—and equally important—our desserts and baked goods are bursting with fresh, wholesome ingredients full of vitamins, minerals, and fiber. They actually are good for you!

How did a couple of doctors come to write a cookbook? The path leading to this book began about ten years ago in Hawaii. We were both attending the same medical conference, and one afternoon found ourselves discussing our common belief in proper diet and exercise and the apparent dichotomy between it and fine food. Since medical school days, Marv had the nickname Dr. Cookie because of his penchant for baking. He partly supported himself in those days by working at a local bakery. Later, as a surgeon in Vietnam, he battled both terror and boredom (two common side effects of war) by manning the ovens at the local mess during off hours. By the time we first met, he was well known at the hospital and among his friends for his healthful cookies and tireless enthusiasm for experimenting with ingredients and techniques.

Steve, on the other hand, had no experience in the kitchen but had lots of experience at the table. He openly admits that his culinary specialty is eating and critiquing. Together, under the tropical sun of Hawaii, we decided to establish Dr. Cookie, Inc.

Our first break came when we secured a contract with Pacific Southwest Airlines to supply it with 30,000 cookies a week. Soon our fledgling company was supplying other airlines with cookies, had established a mail-order business, and had attracted several corporate clients. The company today, managed by Steve's daughter-in-law, Gail Yarnall, is expanding into retail and catalog sales.

Both of us practice medicine full time. Marv practices emergency medicine in Bellingham, Washington, and is on the clinical faculty of the University of Washington. Steve practices cardiology in Edmonds, Washington, and is also on the clinical faculty of the University of Washington.

The cookie company is a sideline and a passion. We support it because we believe in the value of good food and outrageously good desserts that are healthful, too. The recipes in our book are not reproductions of the cookies manufactured commercially by Dr. Cookie, Inc., but are presented in the same spirit. They are all low in fat and have relatively few calories. Most derive far less than 30 percent of total calories from fat. Many are almost fat-free. We use ingredients that increase the fiber content of the desserts and baked goods, we stay away from processed foods, and we select fruits and vegetables full of vitamins and minerals. We never sacrifice flavor!

## Our Philosophy

We sum up our philosophy for maintaining your general health with two phrases: "Know thyself" and "It depends."

Many foods are healthful in general but can be harmful to certain people. For example, about 15 percent of the population has lactase deficiency, which means these are people who cannot digest the milk sugar lactose. When they eat dairy products they are apt to feel gas, bloating, abdominal cramps, sweating, and general malaise. Many lactose-intolerant people can tolerate yogurt.

Some people are gluten sensitive. When they eat bread made with wheat flour or other gluten-containing foods, they can develop an uncomfortable intestinal problem referred to as sprue.

Salt can be a problem for some folks. In general, too much has been said about salt; most of us can tolerate a reasonable amount of salt because the kidneys, given enough water, simply eliminate excess. But people with heart or kidney failure or salt-sensitive hypertension (about 15 percent of all hypertension) should limit salt.

These three examples show how important it is to know what your own body can and cannot tolerate. Most of us can drink a glass of milk with no problem and benefit from the calcium and other nutrients. But if you feel crampy or nauseated after drinking milk, try going without dairy products for a week or so. Feel better? Talk with your doctor. You may have an intestinal lactase deficiency. Try the same test with a gluten-free diet if you suspect you suffer from sprue. Talk with your doctor. But remember, you are the only person who can really, really know how you feel. "Know thyself."

How much of certain foods to eat or which foods to avoid depends on many factors. Too little attention to your diet is not good, but diet anxiety that causes stress is bad. Too little fiber is associated with many health problems, but too much causes gas! We all need essential fatty acids, but too much fat is unhealthy. Too much of vitamins A and D can be dangerous, but we may benefit from many times the RDA for vitamins C and E. These and similar considerations figure into our "It depends" theory of life.

## How to Plan Your Overall Diet

People have developed an unhealthy fear of eating. When eating becomes a chore rather than a pleasure, you lose a glorious part of life. Maintaining a healthful diet can be fun and never has to be deprivation driven. Do not measure your intake bite by bite, but look at the entire week or month. If you eat an average of 14,000 calories a week, it really does not matter if you consume 3,000 one day and 1,000 the next as long as your weekly average remains static.

The same can be said about the amount of fat you ingest. Although we supply the percentage of calories from fat in each recipe, we do not recommend you become addicted to counting fat this way. The percentage of total fat in relationship to calories can be altered in a flash by adding sugar or another source of fat-free calories. Just as for calories, you should heed the *total* grams of fat consumed over a period of time.

Don't consider fat with a bite-by-bite mentality, but be aware of how much you eat every day and every week. Read labels and use your common sense. You will be amazed at how easy it is to reduce fat in the diet, and how little you miss it. Cut back on oils, margarine, hard cheeses, and ice cream. Use yogurt, cottage cheese, and skim milk. Increase your intake of vegetables (try them with lemon juice instead of butter), fruit, and legumes. Try eating more fish and poultry than red meat. You've heard all this before, but it works. You'll feel better and be healthier. And you won't feel deprived.

Finally, don't grit your teeth and swear off desserts. There is no need! Enjoying life is as important for good health as eating right. Stress and pent-up anger contribute as much to ill health as cream and eggs. Take a sensible approach by trying our recipes. We promise, you won't feel deprived. Be happy. Enjoy yourself. Eat dessert. Please.

## The Role of Sugar and Fats

Interestingly, babies are born with an attraction to sweet foods. This is possibly a protective mechanism against rancid or putrid foods, but the fact is that a crying baby sometimes can be quieted by a small amount of sweet food. (Warning: don't feed your baby honey; he or she can't digest it.) What's more, studies by Dr. Judith Wurtman, a brain chemistry researcher at MIT, show that complex carbohydrates—sugar is a simple carbohydrate—relieve acute emotional symptoms of PMS as effectively as tranquilizers. The theory is that carbs lead to increased levels of brain serotonin, which acts like a tranquilizer. We mention these two facts as a way of explaining why so many people feel better and more satisfied after eating something sweet.

As encouraging as this is, we urge moderation. Don't fill your infant with ice cream or shovel chocolate croissants in your mouth if you suffer from PMS. These foods and many others are high in sugar and full of fat, and while a little fat is necessary for hormonal balance, too much is unnecessary and can lead to obesity and health problems.

Fat adds to a feeling of fullness and delays gastric emptying so that the energy stream of foods into the intestines is prolonged rather than "dumped." Dumping occurs when you eat high-sugar, low-fat foods that send the energy supplied by the food racing into the intestine and the bloodstream, causing "sugar highs" followed by rebound lows (hypoglycemia) with attendant symptoms of light-headedness, sweating, and other unpleasant sensations.

Too much sugar also elevates blood fats, termed triglycerides, which team with cholesterol to plug arteries. A high-sugar diet may also contribute to a common syndrome related to high insulin levels called hyperinsulinemia. Some studies show that this syndrome is a major risk factor for cardiovascular disease. Although a history of high-sugar intake and its relation to cardiovascular disease is not conclusive, why wait for the final results of the scientific research? We say take prudent action now and reduce your consumption.

Americans eat, on average, 128 pounds of sugar a year. There is no denying that sugar is one of our nation's most popular food additives and addictions. The amount of soda and sweet treats we consume is staggering, especially since they provide negligible nutritive value. Sugar provides energy but is of no use in maintaining or building healthy tissues.

And still we crave it and its frequent partner-in-crime, fat. This is one very good reason why we have written this book. We understand the need for, and the pleasure of, dessert. We feel that a little sugar may not only "help the medicine go down," it may (in the form of a well-conceived dessert, quick bread, or muffin) add to the richness of life. What is the point of denying yourself the small indulgence of a good dessert? Just do it the Dr. Cookie way.

## The Cholesterol Question

It is clearly established that blood cholesterol is correlated with atherosclerosis and heart disease. This does not mean that everyone should categorically eliminate foods containing cholesterol from his or her diet.

We remember the not-too-distant days when common medical wisdom dictated that every adult limit his or her daily intake of cholesterol to 300 mg or less. Consider that the average person synthesizes approximately 700 mg of cholesterol every day. For most people, when dietary cholesterol is increased the body simply *makes less* cholesterol. An increase in dietary saturated fats, however, causes the liver to produce more cholesterol of the low-density lipoprotein (LDL) type. This is the so-called bad cholesterol associated with arterial disease.

Cholesterol in the diet has some effect, but the threshold for this effect varies tremendously depending on individual absorption, metabolism, and excretion of cholesterol. We note a case reported in the *New England Journal of Medicine* that describes a man with a blood cholesterol level of under 200 who ate more than twenty eggs a day. Egg yolks, as you know, are very high in cholesterol, containing over 200 mg.

Although LDL is recognized as promoting atherogenesis, it is now acknowledged that high-density lipoprotein (HDL) protects against heart disease. Therefore, an HDL over 40 or 50 is *good*. One of our patients had a total cholesterol of more than 300, but her HDL was 105 and so the 300 was not reason for alarm. Further, this lady was ninety-five years old and came from a family with a history of longevity.

Everyone should get his or her blood tested for cholesterol levels. This means submitting to a triad of blood tests that examine LDL levels as well as HDL and triglyceride levels. You cannot simply go by a single number when determining your cardiac risk. You must weigh the results of all three tests.

When the triad of blood test counts shows *low* HDL (under 35), *high* LDL (over 160), and *high* triglycerides (over 250), there is reason for concern. When this is associated with a family history of premature coronary artery disease, you should definitely consider lifestyle alterations through diet and exercise. Your doctor may also recommend medication. If you are concerned, talk with your doctor and decide together on the best approach to the situation.

Overall, it's a good idea to lower your intake of saturated fats—those that come from animals. Increasing your consumption of fruits, vegetables, whole grains, and legumes helps, too.

There is also some evidence that vitamin C may reduce the risk of coronary heart disease. Vitamin C, along with vitamin E, beta carotene, and other molecules are antioxidants. LDL molecules are oxidized, which is to say altered by free radicals and oxidation in the bloodstream, and appear to be the bad guys. Apparently, antioxidants help stabilize the LDL molecule, making it less harmful.

## Dietary Fiber

We hear a lot about fiber and how important it is for a healthy diet. Yet most Americans still eat a fiber-poor diet, averaging only 10 grams a day. The recommended level of fiber is one gram for every 100 calories. For a 2,400-calorie-a-day diet, this means 24 grams of fiber. As with total calories and fat, you can spread this out over a week or so. Don't panic if you neglect your fiber intake every now and then.

Fiber comes in two forms: soluble and insoluble. Soluble dietary fiber dissolves in water; insoluble does not. Examples of foods high in soluble fiber are apples, corn, carrots, oat bran, and legumes. Examples of foods high in insoluble fiber are blackberries, strawberries, processed wheat bran, pinto beans, pears, and graham crackers. Soluble fiber is linked with reducing levels of LDL cholesterol (see page 6 for more information). Insoluble fiber is credited with reducing the risk of colon cancer. All fiber promotes a feeling of fullness and thus is great for weight control. It is also extremely important for bowel regularity.

If appropriate, read labels to decipher how many grams of fiber are in a product. An apple has about 1.2 grams; a half-cup of prunes has nearly 2 grams; and a cup of whole wheat flour has 15 grams. We figure that a slice of whole wheat bread, as measured in our recipes, has about 2 grams of fiber. Adding two tablespoons of wheat bran to sliced fruit or hot cereal provides 3 extra grams of fiber; an ounce of quick-cooking oats also has 3 grams of fiber. Here's an idea: sprinkle wheat bran on your morning oatmeal and slice up an apple to eat with it. That's more than 7 grams of fiber, and you haven't even eaten lunch!

## Information about Our Recipes

The recipes in the book are formulated for great taste without the explosion of fats and calories found in so many desserts and baked goods. We also use high-fiber foods whenever possible, such as apples, carrots, berries, whole wheat flour, and bran. We consider the vitamin and mineral content of the ingredients, too. For example, beta-carotene, which converts to vitamin A, is important as a guard against many types of cancer, and so we include recipes with carrots, sweet potatoes, and dried apricots—all good sources of beta-carotene.

With each recipe we include a breakdown of the calories and fats per serving. We also calculate the total percentage of calories from fat. We made our calculations from the numbers listed on packages and by using *The Complete Book of Food Counts* by Corinne Netzer. We also used *Nutritive Value of Foods*, published by the U.S. Department of Agriculture.

Figuring the percentage of calories from fat is easy. To do so, multiply the grams of fat per serving by nine. Divide this number by the total calories per serving. Move the decimal point two numbers to the right. That is the percent. For instance, take the Oatmeal-Orange Muffins on page 131. Each serving (one muffin) has 151 calories and 3 grams of fat. Plug this into the formula and you get .18 or 18 percent. Here's the rub. Add a half-cup of brown sugar to the recipe. The muffins are sweeter and now contain 184 calories each. Use the formula and you find that the percentage of calories from fat is 15 percent. Does that make them more healthful? You decide!

## The Ingredients We Use

We're fortunate to live in the lush, fertile Pacific Northwest. We have some of the best apples, berries, peaches, and garden vegetables in the country. Both our families take full advantage of this, eagerly anticipating the arrival of each season's best products. We can't wait for June's first strawberries, July's blueberries and raspberries, August's peaches and tomatoes, September's zucchini and early apples. You get the idea. We prefer organically grown produce, and we urge everyone to seek it out if possible. It may not look as perfect as that grown with the aid of pesticides, herbicides, and chemical fertilizers, but it *tastes* so much better. Use fresh fruits and vegetables in our recipes whenever possible—unless otherwise instructed—and try to cook with those that are in season in your region. They most likely will taste better than imported produce and certainly will be less expensive.

Most of the ingredients for our recipes are available in the local grocery store or supermarket. If not, they probably can be found in natural foods stores. We have noticed a heartening trend in the past few years in that many of the products we used to find only in natural foods stores are showing up in supermarkets. To us, this spells progress.

**Dairy Products** You will find a lot of low-fat and skim milk in our recipes. We also rely heavily on low-fat and nonfat yogurt. We use buttermilk for its distinctive tang and acidic quality. These dairy products help make baked goods tender and moist. They also provide calcium and vitamins A, $B_{12}$, $B_6$, and D in good amounts. We avoid full-fat dairy products and never use butter. Who needs the saturated fat?

We find yogurt to be a useful substitute for high-fat ingredients such as cream and sour cream. We use only gelatin-free yogurt, usually buying Dannon and Yoplait, but any brand is fine as long as it has no gelatin. Yogurt containing live cultures has beneficial bacteria that can be helpful to ulcers, bowel disorders, and for some, vaginitis. What's more, many people with lactose intolerance can eat yogurt containing live cultures. Evidently, the bacteria complete part of the digestive process, making the yogurt easier to digest.

We suggest frozen yogurt instead of ice cream or ice milk every time. Three-quarters of a cup of gourmet ice cream contains more than 400 calories, 60 percent of which comes from fat. With ice milk, the calorie count drops to 150 and the percentage of calories from fat to 20 percent. Three-quarters of a cup of frozen yogurt has about 135 calories and only 10 percent is derived from fat. If you crave a frozen dessert and want no fat, try fruit sorbet. A cup contains 180 calories but zero fat.

Cheese is a problem for many people trying to maintain a low-fat diet. It's hard to resist. As a population, we consume about twenty-six pounds of cheese per person per year. We like a good, sharp cheddar as much as the next person, but because cheddar is 70 percent fat, we limit our intake, and when we eat it, we slice it very thin.

The kind of cheese makes a difference. Most firm cheeses, such as cheddar, Swiss, and Monterey jack, are high in fat. Creamy cheeses are, too. Camembert is 81 percent fat; blue cheese is 72 percent fat. We attack this problem by avoiding cheese much of the time and at other times using low-fat alternatives such as low-fat ricotta, cottage cheese, part-skim cheddar, and part-skim mozzarella.

**Eggs** Yes, we use eggs in some recipes. Eggs have taken a bad rap in recent years, and while the yolks do contain about 200 mg of cholesterol and 7 grams of fat, one egg in a recipe that feeds six people is not so bad. Plus, egg yolks are good sources of vitamin A, biotin, and essential fatty acids. Eggs are wonderful emulsifiers and add significantly to the texture of the final product. We use lots of egg whites, which are fat-free and cholesterol-free, and so are essentially blameless in the egg controversy. Egg whites lighten and leaven baked preparations. They're also wonderful for protein.

You might ask why we don't use egg substitutes. Certainly there is a wide choice of them on the market. We decided that while they don't alter the flavor of the baked good and do provide the glutinous properties of eggs, they are a little more complicated to buy and more expensive than the real thing. Food technology changes quickly and the egg substitute you use today may be gone or improved upon tomorrow. Eggs will always be with us. It's simpler (and less costly) to stay with eggs and egg whites.

**Fats** We have already addressed the issue of fats. When it comes to this slippery question, we have to say, "It depends." A little fat is not bad. You have to gauge your intake of fat over time and, if you overindulge one day, moderate the next. But the fact remains that most baked goods and desserts cannot be made without some fat.

Whenever possible, we use vegetable oil rather than margarine. (We never use butter.) Our oils of choice are canola, corn, and olive. Canola and olive are high in omega-3 unsaturated fatty acids, which have been shown to lower LDL cholesterol levels without lowering HDL cholesterol levels. Olive oil is king in this area and has also been shown to lower blood pressure, help regulate blood glucose, and provide additional benefits as an antioxidant. The problem is, olive oil has a very distinctive flavor that rarely tastes good in desserts and baked goods. Canola oil is almost as good and is virtually tasteless.

All oils are 100 percent fat. Each gram of fat contains 9 calories. A tablespoon of fat contains 15 grams of fat, which equals 135 calories. Use oils judiciously.

We use margarine in some recipes because, quite frankly, it sometimes bakes better than oil. But overall we avoid it. While margarine is made from an unsaturated liquid source, during the transformation from liquid to solid it loses some of its beneficial effects. Further, it recently has been reported that margarine contains a certain level of transfatty acids. These seem to cause an increase in lipid metabolism and possibly in cholesterol and triglycerides.

**Flour** We learned in our hippie days during the 1960s and early 1970s that whole wheat and other whole-grain flours were more "healthy." Back then, we shunned "white" flour and, using only whole-grain flours, produced cookies and breads that may have tasted okay but were often as heavy as a trunk full of love beads. Over the years we realized that white flour is not the villain we once thought it to be. True, it's been stripped of the healthful parts of the grain—the germ and the bran—but the light, starchy endosperm that's left behind is a powerful source of gluten and is not weighted down by the germ and bran.

We use unbleached all-purpose flour in most recipes. We never use bleached flour, which has been treated with chemicals and has no culinary, or other, advantage over unbleached. Unbleached all-purpose flour provides good texture and pleasing lightness. When possible, we combine it with whole wheat or another whole-grain flour such as rye. We sometimes toss in a little oat or wheat bran for increased fiber. Oat bran may also reduce elevated LDL levels.

In a few recipes we call for cake flour. Cake flour is milled from softer wheat than all-purpose flour and produces a more tender final product. If a recipe calls for cake flour, please use it. Keep in mind that some brands of cake flour are "self-rising," which means they are mixed with leaveners. We never use self-rising cake flour.

Finally, we rely heavily on rolled oats as a dry ingredient. Their flavor is excellent, their fiber content is even better, and the texture of the final product is wonderful. In the recipes we specify whether you should use regular oats (old-fashioned) or quick-cooking oats. We do not use instant oatmeal.

**Nuts** Nuts are one of nature's gifts. Some, like almonds, hazelnuts, and pistachios, are rich sources of monounsaturated fat such as oleic acid, a useful antioxidant. Most are high, too, in omega-3 fatty acids, also antioxidants. Their high vitamin E content is valuable in the fight against heart disease and some cancers. Properties in all nuts battle arterial disease and even degenerative diseases such as Parkinson's.

Almonds are especially good. They are low in saturated fat and are full of vegetable protein and fiber. They have been shown to lower blood cholesterol in humans and tend to stabilize blood sugar and insulin levels. They also contain some anticancer compounds.

Nuts add great flavor and crunch to all manner of desserts and baked goods. They're easily available most of the year and are terrific for snacking. What's not to like about nuts? They are very high in fat. We add them to recipes often as an optional ingredient, suggesting you use them for their flavor and texture unless doing so adds too much fat to your weekly diet. When the nuts are optional, we list the difference in calories and fat in the specific recipe. You have to make the decision depending on your weekly intake of fat and calories. "Know thyself."

*Sweeteners* We have already explained our position on sugar, and while we deplore excessive sugar consumption, a little sugar is not a bad thing. It's absolutely necessary in most desserts. We use granulated white sugar in small amounts, and when possible use brown sugar. Brown sugar adds a delicious caramel flavor to baked goods. Both light and dark brown sugar work equally well in our recipes.

We also use honey and, to a lesser extent, molasses. Gram for gram, honey and sugar contain the same number of calories, but honey is more intensely sweet and sometimes less goes further. Its consistency does not work in every recipe, however, and we found in baking that sugar was generally more satisfactory. Molasses provides rich, earthy sweetness that works best with other earthy flavors such as whole wheat and oats.

## Enjoy the Book—Enjoy Your Life

Long ago we came to realize that life was meant to be lived! We work hard and play hard. We eat prudently but well and happily. We do not overindulge, nor do we deprive ourselves of life's relatively harmless pleasures— such as dessert!

We believe that dessert and baked goods can be incorporated into a healthful life as easily as following our recipes. Once you grasp our philosophy of baking and cooking, after trying a few of our recipes, you will be able to modify your own favorite, high-fat desserts to reduce the fat in them. What a shame it would be for a chocolate lover never to eat it again! How sad for a pie or cake fan to stop eating these treats.

Food is not bad. Overall, it is very good. It nurtures the body, surely, but just as important it feeds the spirit. We should enjoy it sensibly but without guilt, without stress.

Go ahead. Eat dessert. Please!

# Chapter 1

# Cookies

$D$r. Cookie began with cookies—those simple everyday treats that we both have always loved. To us, the phrase "cookies with milk" is as comforting as a hug from mom. So, with the establishment of the Dr. Cookie business, we hoped to nurture folks with cookies that were undeniably low in fat and calories. In this chapter, we offer homemade cookies equally low in fat and calories that taste as good as those high-fat cookies you probably grew up with.

In our commercial cookie business we use an all-natural fat substitute from Pfizer Pharmaceutical Company called Litess. It's not available at the grocery store and therefore it was not practical to use it for the cookies in our book. Instead, we developed recipes using ingredients anyone can find at the neighborhood supermarket, such as all-purpose and whole wheat flour, rolled oats, dried fruit, orange and lemon rind, brown sugar, and nuts. And we sneak in chocolate chips whenever possible.

We have far more recipes in this chapter than in any other. But that's how it should be. We are proud of our other recipes. They taste great. But we are simply crazy about cookies. So pour a glass of milk (low-fat, naturally!), grab a few cookies, and enjoy yourself! Invite your mom to join you.

*An apple a day won't keep Dr. Cookie away. We think apples are among the best foods going. They aid digestion and some studies indicate that they help control cholesterol. We've combined apples with other healthful ingredients in these winning cookies.*

- 1½ cups shredded unpeeled apple (about 1 medium apple)
- ¼ cup unsweetened apple juice
- ½ cup granulated sugar
- ¾ cup dried cranberries or raisins
- 1 large egg
- ½ cup packed brown sugar
- 1 teaspoon vanilla extract
- ¼ cup vegetable oil
- 1 cup unbleached all-purpose flour
- ½ cup rye flour
- 1½ cups quick-cooking multigrain cereal, such as Quaker
- 1 teaspoon baking powder
- 1 teaspoon baking soda
- 2 teaspoons pumpkin pie spice

Preheat the oven to 350°F. and coat 2 baking sheets with nonstick cooking spray.

Combine the shredded apple, apple juice, granulated sugar, and cranberries. Set aside.

Beat the egg, brown sugar, vanilla, and oil with an electric mixer until smooth. Add the shredded apple mixture and stir it into the batter by hand. Add the flours, cereal, baking powder, baking soda, and pie spice and stir into the batter by hand. Let the batter sit for about 5 minutes to absorb all the liquid.

Drop the batter by rounded teaspoonfuls about 2 inches apart onto the baking sheets and bake for 10 to 12 minutes or until the cookies are lightly browned. Cool on a wire rack. Repeat until all the cookies are baked.

# Apple Cookies

**Yield:** about 60 cookies

**Calories per cookie:** 48

**Fat per cookie:** 1.2 grams

**Percent of calories from fat:** 21%

# Dr. Cookie's Applesauce Nut Cookies

**Yield:** about 48 cookies

**Calories per cookie:** 64

**Fat per cookie:** 2 grams

**Percent of calories from fat:** 28%

*The applesauce makes these spicy cookies especially moist and the nuts make them crunchy.*

1 large egg
1 cup packed brown sugar
¼ cup vegetable oil
1 cup natural unsweetened applesauce
1½ cups unbleached all-purpose flour
½ cup whole wheat flour
1½ teaspoons baking soda
1 teaspoon ground cinnamon
½ teaspoon grated nutmeg
½ teaspoon ground cloves
¼ teaspoon salt
1 cup raisins
½ cup chopped walnuts

Preheat the oven to 350°F. and coat 2 baking sheets with nonstick cooking spray.

Beat the egg, brown sugar, and oil with an electric mixer until smooth. Add the applesauce and beat again just until blended. Add the flours, baking soda, spices, and salt and beat until well mixed. Stir in the raisins and walnuts.

Drop the batter by rounded teaspoonfuls about 2 inches apart onto the baking sheets and bake for 10 to 15 minutes or until the cookies are lightly browned. Cool on a wire rack. Repeat until all the cookies are baked.

These soft, chewy, old-fashioned cookies are a good example of how successfully two egg whites can be substituted for every whole egg in many recipes.

4 large egg whites
1 cup packed brown sugar
2 cups natural unsweetened applesauce
1 teaspoon vanilla extract
2 cups unbleached all-purpose flour
2 cups old-fashioned rolled oats
1 teaspoon baking soda
1½ teaspoons ground cinnamon
½ cup chopped dates

Preheat the oven to 350°F. and coat 2 baking sheets with nonstick cooking spray.

Beat the egg whites and brown sugar with an electric mixer until smooth. Add the applesauce and vanilla, and beat again just until blended. Add the flour, oats, baking soda, and cinnamon and beat until well mixed. Add the dates and stir to combine.

Drop the batter by rounded teaspoonfuls about 2 inches apart onto the baking sheets and bake for 12 to 15 minutes or until the cookies are lightly browned. Cool on a wire rack. Repeat until all the cookies are baked.

# Applesauce Oatmeal Cookies

Yield: 48 cookies

Calories per cookie: 58

Fat per cookie: .2 gram

Percent of calories from fat: 3%

# Apricot Drops

Yield: 24 cookies

Calories per cookie: 71

Fat per cookie: 1.4 grams

Percent of calories from fat: 18%

*Why do we love these cookies? Because of the richness provided by the dried apricots. Also because in the fruit kingdom, apricots are surpassed only by cantaloupes as a terrific source of beta-carotene, which the body converts to vitamin A. If the apricots stick to your knife during chopping, put them in the freezer for a few minutes. The cold will make them less sticky.*

1 large egg

⅔ cup packed brown sugar

2 tablespoons vegetable oil

1 tablespoon orange juice

1 cup unbleached all-purpose flour

1 teaspoon baking powder

1 teaspoon grated orange rind

¼ teaspoon salt

1 cup coarsely chopped dried apricots

Preheat the oven to 350°F. and coat 2 baking sheets with nonstick cooking spray.

Beat the egg, brown sugar, oil, and orange juice with an electric mixer until smooth. Add the flour, baking powder, orange rind, and salt and beat until well mixed. Add the apricots and stir to combine.

Drop the batter by rounded teaspoonfuls about 2 inches apart onto the baking sheets and bake for 10 to 12 minutes or until the cookies are lightly browned. Cool on a wire rack. Repeat, if necessary, until all the cookies are baked.

Bananas are an excellent source of dietary fiber and potassium, both of which are essential for a healthy diet. We rely on mashed bananas to replace half the fat that was in the original Dr. Cookie recipe for these moist, chewy cookies. These taste just as good—maybe even better!

1 large egg

1 cup packed brown sugar

¼ cup vegetable oil

1½ cups mashed ripe bananas (about 3 bananas)

½ teaspoon vanilla extract

1½ cups unbleached all-purpose flour

1½ cups old-fashioned rolled oats

1 teaspoon baking soda

1 teaspoon ground cinnamon

¼ teaspoon grated nutmeg

½ cup chopped walnuts or semisweet chocolate chips

Preheat the oven to 350°F. and coat 2 baking sheets with nonstick cooking spray.

Beat the egg, brown sugar, and oil with an electric mixer until smooth. Add the bananas and beat again. Add the vanilla, flour, oats, baking soda, cinnamon, and nutmeg and beat until well mixed. Stir in the nuts or chocolate chips. Let the batter sit for about 5 minutes so that the oats can absorb the liquid.

Drop the batter by rounded teaspoonfuls about 2 inches apart onto the baking sheets and bake for 12 to 15 minutes or until the cookies are lightly browned. Cool on a wire rack. Repeat until all the cookies are baked.

# Banana Surprise Cookies

Yield: 48 cookies

Calories per cookie:
65 (with nuts or chips)

Fat per cookie:
2 grams (with nuts or chips)

Percent of calories from fat:
28% (with nuts or chips)

# Carrot Cookies

Yield: 48 cookies

Calories per cookie: 48

Fat per cookie: 1.3 grams

Percent of calories from fat: 24%

**W**hat's up doc? Carrots in cookies? Why not? As they do for carrot cake, shredded carrots give rich flavor and pleasing moistness to cookies. What's more, they are good for you as a rich source of beta-carotene.

1 large egg

½ cup packed brown sugar

½ cup granulated sugar

¼ cup vegetable oil

1 teaspoon vanilla extract

¾ cup shredded carrot (about 1 large carrot)

1 cup unbleached all-purpose flour

1 cup quick-cooking oats (not instant) or quick-cooking multigrain cereal, such as Quaker

1 teaspoon baking powder

1 teaspoon ground cinnamon

½ teaspoon grated nutmeg

¼ teaspoon salt

1 cup raisins

Preheat the oven to 375°F. and coat 2 baking sheets with nonstick cooking spray.

Beat the egg, sugars, oil, and vanilla extract with an electric mixer until smooth. Add the shredded carrot and beat again. Add the flour, oats, baking powder, cinnamon, nutmeg, and salt and beat until well mixed. Add the raisins and stir to combine.

Drop the batter by rounded teaspoonfuls about 2 inches apart onto the baking sheets and bake for 10 to 12 minutes or until the cookies are lightly browned. Cool on a wire rack. Repeat until all the cookies are baked.

Chocolate chip cookies are an American institution, and these deserve a place in the cookie hall of fame. They taste just as rich and chocolaty as you could want, but won't take a toll on your waistline. Use these in our recipe for Dr. Cookie's Cookies 'n Cream Frozen Pie on page 96.

6 tablespoons (¾ stick) margarine

⅔ cup packed brown sugar

⅔ cup granulated sugar

2 large eggs

¼ cup skim milk

1½ teaspoons vanilla extract

3¼ cups unbleached all-purpose flour

1½ teaspoons baking soda

¼ teaspoon salt

¾ cup semisweet chocolate chips

Preheat the oven to 350°F. and coat 2 baking sheets with nonstick cooking spray.

Beat the margarine and sugars with an electric mixer until smooth. Add the eggs and beat again. Add the milk and vanilla and beat again until smooth. Add the flour, baking soda, and salt and beat until well mixed. Add the chocolate chips and stir to combine.

Drop the batter by rounded teaspoonfuls about 2 inches apart onto the baking sheets. These cookies do not spread very much during baking so you might choose to flatten each one slightly with your fingertips or the back of a teaspoon. Bake for 10 to 12 minutes or until the cookies are lightly browned. Cool on a wire rack. Repeat until all the cookies are baked.

OFFICIALLY NOTE:

# Dr. Cookie's Chocolate Chip Cookies

Yield: 48 cookies

Calories per cookie: 78

Fat per cookie: 2.5 grams

Percent of calories from fat: 29%

# Heavenly Chocolate Oatmeal Cookies

**Yield:** 48 cookies

**Calories per cookie:** 50

**Fat per cookie:** 1.5 grams

**Percent of calories from fat:** 27%

*F*or those days when you need chocolate—as opposed to those days when you simply want chocolate—we suggest trying a batch of these. You won't be disappointed. We took most of the fat out of the cookies, but boosted the chocolate flavor by adding a teaspoonful of chocolate extract. This delicious "secret ingredient" is sold in most supermarkets near the vanilla and almond extracts.

1 large egg

½ cup packed brown sugar

½ cup granulated sugar

¼ cup vegetable oil

¼ cup low-fat gelatin-free vanilla or coffee yogurt

1 teaspoon vanilla extract

1 teaspoon chocolate extract

1 cup quick-cooking oats (not instant)

½ cup cocoa powder

1⅛ cups unbleached all-purpose flour

½ teaspoon baking powder

½ teaspoon baking soda

¼ teaspoon salt

Preheat the oven to 350°F. and coat 2 baking sheets with nonstick cooking spray.

Beat the egg, sugars, and oil with an electric mixer until smooth. Add the yogurt, vanilla and chocolate extracts, oats, and cocoa powder and beat again. Add the flour, baking powder, baking soda, and salt and beat until well mixed. Let the batter sit for about 10 minutes so that the oats can absorb the liquid.

Drop the batter by rounded teaspoonfuls about 2 inches apart onto the baking sheets and bake for 7 to 8 minutes or until the cookies are slightly puffy and no longer look wet. Cool on a wire rack. Repeat until all the cookies are baked.

We call these "power" cookies because they combine caffeine (in the coffee and the cocoa), prunes, and oats. Adding the chocolate chips may seem like overkill, but for a burst of chocolate flavor, stir them into the batter. Either way, the cookies are great.

½ cup pitted prunes
½ cup very hot (not boiling) water
½ cup quick-cooking oats (not instant)
1 cup unbleached all-purpose flour
1 cup cocoa powder
½ teaspoon baking soda
1 teaspoon instant coffee granules
¼ teaspoon salt
1 large egg
½ cup nonfat gelatin-free plain yogurt
¼ cup vegetable oil
¾ cup packed brown sugar
¾ cup granulated sugar
½ cup semisweet chocolate chips (optional)

Preheat the oven to 350°F. and coat 2 baking sheets with nonstick cooking spray.

Soak the prunes in the hot water for about 10 minutes. Puree the prunes and any hot water not absorbed by them in a blender until smooth. Stir the oats into the puree and set aside.

Whisk the flour, cocoa, baking soda, coffee granules, and salt together until well mixed. Make sure the cocoa is lump free.

Beat the egg, yogurt, oil, and sugars with an electric mixer until smooth. Add the prune-oatmeal mixture and the dry ingredients and beat until well mixed. Stir the chocolate chips into the batter, if using.

Drop the batter by rounded teaspoonfuls about 2 inches apart onto the baking sheets and bake for 10 to 12 minutes or until the cookies are slightly firm to the touch. Cool on a wire rack. Repeat until all the cookies are baked.

# Chocolate Power-Burst Cookies

**Yield:** 48 cookies

**Calories per cookie:**
56 without chocolate chips;
65 with chocolate chips

**Fat per cookie:**
1.4 grams without chocolate chips; 2 grams with chocolate chips

**Percent of calories from fat:**
23% without chocolate chips;
28% with chocolate chips

# Gingerbread Drops

**Yield:** 48 cookies

**Calories per cookie:** 50

**Fat per cookie:** 1.5 grams

**Percent of calories from fat:** 27%

Gingerbread is an all-American favorite, and these soft, cakelike cookies are a good way to savor a little without overindulging. What's more, ginger is good for you—research indicates that even in small amounts, it helps lower blood cholesterol. Can't hurt to try, especially since it tastes so good.

1 large egg
⅓ cup packed brown sugar
½ cup molasses
¼ cup vegetable oil
½ cup buttermilk
1½ cups unbleached all-purpose flour
½ cup wheat germ
1 teaspoon baking powder
1 teaspoon baking soda
1 teaspoon ground cinnamon
1 teaspoon ground ginger
¼ teaspoon salt
¾ cup raisins

Preheat the oven to 350°F. and coat 2 baking sheets with nonstick cooking spray.

Beat the egg, brown sugar, molasses, and oil with an electric mixer until smooth. Add the buttermilk and beat again. Add the flour, wheat germ, baking powder, baking soda, cinnamon, ginger, and salt and beat until well mixed. Stir the raisins into the batter.

Drop the batter by rounded teaspoonfuls about 2 inches apart onto the baking sheets and bake for 12 to 14 minutes or until the cookies are lightly browned. Cool on a wire rack. Repeat until all the cookies are baked.

We named these cookies for the harvest because, to our way of thinking, they contain the wonderful flavors of autumn: cinnamon, nutmeg, nuts, pumpkin, and apple. They also have a half-cup of oat bran, a mostly soluble fiber that is a good source of B vitamins and, when part of a balanced diet, can help maintain healthful levels of cholesterol in the blood.

1 large egg
1 cup packed brown sugar
¼ cup vegetable oil
1 cup unsweetened pumpkin puree
1½ cups unbleached all-purpose flour
½ cup oat bran
1 teaspoon baking soda
1 teaspoon baking powder
1 teaspoon ground cinnamon
½ teaspoon grated nutmeg
¼ teaspoon salt
¾ cup raisins
¼ cup chopped walnuts
1 cup finely chopped unpeeled apple (about 1 large apple)

Preheat the oven to 350°F. and coat 2 baking sheets with nonstick cooking spray.

Beat the egg, brown sugar, and oil with an electric mixer until smooth. Add the pumpkin and beat again. Add the flour, oat bran, baking soda, baking powder, cinnamon, nutmeg, and salt and beat until well mixed. Stir the raisins, walnuts, and apple into the batter.

Drop the batter by rounded teaspoonfuls about 2 inches apart onto the baking sheets and bake for 12 to 14 minutes or until the cookies are lightly browned. Cool on a wire rack. Repeat until all the cookies are baked.

# Harvest Cookies

Yield: 48 cookies

Calories per cookie: 57

Fat per cookie: 1.8 grams

Percent of calories from fat: 28%

# Hippie Cookies

**Yield:** 36 cookies

**Calories per cookie:** 78

**Fat per cookie:** 2.6 grams

**Percent of calories from fat:** 30%

Remember the sixties when health foods were "big"? They're even more popular now, but no longer the novelty they were back then. Today, most cooks are more sophisticated in their use of these wonderful products. In those days we never baked with sugar, always used whole-grain flours, and added seeds and fruit and who knows what else to every batch of cookies. Of course, we also wore tie-dye shirts and love beads. Today, we appreciate the trend toward lighter baking, but this is a sixties recipe that has stayed with us over the years and one that we adapted to fit into our nineties lives. Peace.

1 large egg
¾ cup honey
¼ cup vegetable oil
½ cup skim milk
2 cups rye flour
1 teaspoon baking powder
1½ teaspoons pumpkin pie spice
¼ teaspoon salt
½ cup raisins
½ cup ¼-inch dried apple bits
3 tablespoons sunflower seeds
¼ cup sesame seeds

Preheat the oven to 350°F. and coat 2 baking sheets with nonstick cooking spray.

Beat the egg, honey, oil, and milk with an electric mixer until smooth. Add the flour, baking powder, pie spice, and salt and beat until well mixed. Stir the raisins, dried apples, sunflower seeds, and sesame seeds into the batter.

Drop the batter by rounded teaspoonfuls about 2 inches apart onto the baking sheets and bake for 10 to 12 minutes or until the cookies are lightly browned. Cool on a wire rack. Repeat until all the cookies are baked.

We love the flavor combination of orange and poppy seeds, and have made these cookies extra light by substituting low-fat cream cheese for lots of butter or margarine. But be sure to use low-fat cheese, not a nonfat cream cheese spread. For even lighter cookies, use two cups of cake flour (not self-rising) instead of the all-purpose flour.

1  large egg
1  large egg white
1  cup sugar
2  tablespoons vegetable oil
½  cup low-fat cream cheese
1  tablespoon orange juice
2  teaspoons grated orange rind
1¾ cups unbleached all-purpose flour
½  teaspoon baking soda
¼  teaspoon salt
2  tablespoons poppy seeds

Preheat the oven to 350°F. and coat 2 baking sheets with nonstick cooking spray.

Beat the egg, egg white, sugar, and oil with an electric mixer until smooth. Add the cream cheese, orange juice, and orange rind and be_ again. Add the flour, baking soda, salt, and poppy seeds and beat until v mixed.

Drop the batter by rounded teaspoonfuls about 2 inches apart or _ne baking sheets and bake for 10 to 12 minutes or until the cookies ar _ghtly browned. Cool on a wire rack. Repeat until all the cookies are b_ _.

# Orange— Poppy Seed Cookies

**Yield:** 48 cookies

**Calories per cookie:**

**Fat per cookie:** 1_ _ms

**Percent of cal_ _rom fat:** 27%

31

# Peanut Butter— Banana Cookies

**Yield:** 40 cookies

**Calories per cookie:** 57

**Fat per cookie:** 1.8 grams

**Percent of calories from fat:** 28%

These cookies remind us of the peanut butter and banana sandwiches we loved when we were kids. Plus, bananas supply potassium and other important minerals, and their natural sweetness means we do not add much sugar to the recipe.

1 large egg
½ cup natural crunchy-style peanut butter
½ cup mashed ripe banana (about 1 banana)
½ cup packed brown sugar
½ cup granulated sugar
1¼ cups unbleached all-purpose flour
½ teaspoon baking soda
½ teaspoon baking powder

Preheat the oven to 350°F. and coat 2 baking sheets with nonstick cooking spray.

Beat the egg, peanut butter, banana, and sugars with an electric mixer until smooth. Add the flour, baking soda, and baking powder and beat until well mixed.

Drop the batter by rounded teaspoonfuls about 2 inches apart onto the baking sheets and bake for 10 to 12 minutes or until the cookies are lightly browned. (For a classic peanut butter cookie appearance, flatten each cookie with the tines of a fork just before baking.) Cool on the cookie sheet for 2 minutes and then cool completely on a wire rack. Repeat until all the cookies are baked.

*Peanut butter gets 83 percent of its calories from fat and so it's challenging to create a low-fat peanut butter cookie. But peanut butter is also a good source of protein—and it tastes yummy. Therefore, with a nod or two to health, we think it's fine to splurge every now and again. And these are worth the splurge!*

1 large egg

1 large egg white

⅔ cup packed brown sugar

2 tablespoons vegetable oil

½ cup natural creamy-style peanut butter

½ teaspoon vanilla extract

1 cup unbleached all-purpose flour

½ cup old-fashioned rolled oats

½ teaspoon baking soda

Preheat the oven to 350°F. and coat 2 baking sheets with nonstick cooking spray.

Beat the egg, egg white, brown sugar, oil, peanut butter, and vanilla with an electric mixer until smooth. Add the flour, oats, and baking soda and beat until well mixed.

Drop the batter by rounded teaspoonfuls about 2 inches apart onto the baking sheets and bake for 12 to 15 minutes or until the cookies are lightly browned. Cool on a wire rack. Repeat until all the cookies are baked.

# Peanut Butter— Oatmeal Cookies

Yield: 24 cookies

Calories per cookie: 92

Fat per cookie: 4.5 grams

Percent of calories from fat: 44%

# Prune-Oatmeal Cookies

**Yield:** 48 cookies

**Calories per cookie:** 67

**Fat per cookie:** 1.4 grams

**Percent of calories from fat:** 19%

M*ama always said to eat your prunes, didn't she? She was right (as usual). Prunes are an important source of fiber and, when combined with the rolled oats in this recipe, make cookies that are so fiber-rich we were tempted to dub them "Get Regular Goodies."*

¼ cup whole pitted prunes, plus ¾ cup chopped pitted prunes

¼ cup very hot (not boiling) water

1 large egg

2 large egg whites

1¼ cups packed brown sugar

¼ cup vegetable oil

1 teaspoon vanilla extract

1½ cups unbleached all-purpose flour

2 cups old-fashioned rolled oats

1 teaspoon baking soda

¼ teaspoon salt

Preheat the oven to 350°F. and coat 2 baking sheets with nonstick cooking spray.

Soak the whole prunes in the hot water for about 10 minutes. Puree the prunes and any hot water not absorbed by them in a blender until smooth.

Beat the egg, egg whites, brown sugar, oil, and vanilla with an electric mixer until smooth. Add the prune puree and beat again.

Toss the flour with the chopped prunes, making sure the prune pieces do not clump. Add the flour and chopped prunes, oats, baking soda, and salt to the batter and beat until well mixed.

Drop the batter by rounded teaspoonfuls about 2 inches apart onto the baking sheets and bake for 10 to 12 minutes or until the cookies are lightly browned. Cool on a wire rack. Repeat until all the cookies are baked.

These spicy cookies are sweetened with honey and plump, sticky dates, and are moistened with pumpkin puree. Honey is one of the oldest sweeteners known and, for good reason, has maintained its allure over the centuries. Clover honey is the most common, although you can buy lighter tasting orange-blossom or berry honeys. Honey is almost twice as sweet as sugar, although its calorie count, teaspoon for teaspoon, is about the same.

1 large egg

½ cup honey

¼ cup vegetable oil

1 cup unsweetened pumpkin puree

1 cup unbleached all-purpose flour

½ cup whole wheat flour

1 teaspoon baking soda

1 teaspoon baking powder

1 teaspoon ground cinnamon

½ teaspoon grated nutmeg

¼ teaspoon ground cloves

¼ teaspoon salt

1 cup chopped dates

Preheat the oven to 350°F. and coat 2 baking sheets with nonstick cooking spray.

Beat the egg, honey, and oil with an electric mixer until smooth. Add the pumpkin and beat again. Add the flours, baking soda, baking powder, cinnamon, nutmeg, cloves, and salt and beat until well mixed. Stir the dates into the batter.

Drop the batter by rounded teaspoonfuls about 2 inches apart onto the baking sheets and bake for 12 to 14 minutes or until the cookies are lightly browned. Cool on a wire rack. Repeat until all the cookies are baked.

# Pumpkin-Date Drops

Yield: 48 cookies

Calories per cookie: 42

Fat per cookie: 1.3 grams

Percent of calories from fat: 28%

# Tropical Treats

**Yield:** 48 cookies

**Calories per cookie:** 56

**Fat per cookie:** 1.5 grams

**Percent of calories from fat:** 24%

Although we live in the very temperate climate of the Pacific Northwest, we are partial to the tropics. In fact, it was on a tropical beach that the Dr. Cookie dream was first envisioned. We pack these cookies with tropical flavors but not much fat. Dried papaya and pineapple are easy to find in most natural foods stores, and are increasingly available in supermarkets, too. If you can't find unsweetened shredded coconut, use the sweetened kind.

> 2 cups unbleached all-purpose flour
>
> 1 teaspoon baking soda
>
> ¼ teaspoon salt
>
> 1 8-ounce can unsweetened crushed pineapple, undrained
>
> ⅓ cup chopped dried papaya
>
> ⅓ cup chopped dried pineapple
>
> ⅓ cup golden raisins
>
> 1 large egg
>
> 1 cup packed brown sugar
>
> ¼ cup vegetable oil
>
> 1 teaspoon grated orange rind
>
> ¼ cup unsweetened shredded coconut

Preheat the oven to 350°F. and coat 2 baking sheets with nonstick cooking spray.

Whisk together the flour, baking soda, and salt and set aside.

Stir together the canned pineapple, papaya, dried pineapple, and raisins and set aside.

Beat the egg, brown sugar, oil, and orange rind with an electric mixer until smooth. Add the flour mixture and beat again. Add the fruit mixture and beat until well mixed. Stir the coconut into the batter.

Drop the batter by rounded teaspoonfuls about 2 inches apart onto the baking sheets and bake for 10 to 12 minutes or until the cookies are lightly browned. Cool on a wire rack. Repeat until all the cookies are baked.

**T**hese spicy little cookies puff up quickly in the hot oven and must be watched carefully so that they don't overbake. Try replacing ½ cup of all-purpose flour with ½ cup of rye flour for an interesting flavor variation.

3 tablespoons margarine

½ cup packed brown sugar

¼ cup granulated sugar

1 large egg

½ cup nonfat gelatin-free plain yogurt

1 teaspoon vanilla extract

1½ cups unbleached all-purpose flour

¼ teaspoon baking powder

¼ teaspoon baking soda

¾ teaspoon ground cinnamon

½ teaspoon grated nutmeg

¼ teaspoon ground allspice

¼ teaspoon ground cloves

Beat the margarine and sugars with an electric mixer until smooth. Add the egg and beat again. Add the yogurt and vanilla and beat until smooth. Add the flour, baking powder, baking soda, cinnamon, nutmeg, allspice, and cloves and beat until well mixed. Cover the batter and refrigerate for at least 1 hour.

Preheat the oven to 425°F. and coat 2 baking sheets with nonstick cooking spray.

Drop the batter by rounded teaspoonfuls onto the baking sheets. The cookies do not spread much and so may be fairly close together. Bake for 7 to 9 minutes or until the cookies are puffed and lightly browned. Cool on a wire rack. Repeat until all the cookies are baked.

# Spice Puffs

Yield: 48 cookies

Calories per cookie: 34

Fat per cookie: .9 gram

Percent of calories from fat: 17%

# Meringues

**Yield:** 12 large or 24 small meringues

**Calories per meringue:**
36 for large meringues; 18 for small meringues

**Fat per meringue:** 0

**Percent of calories from fat:** 0

Everyone loves meringues, especially children. They are sweet and crunchy and, perhaps best of all, fat-free. Make sure the bowl and beaters of the electric mixer are clean and dry before you attempt to beat the egg whites. We use meringue in a number of our favorite desserts including Pared-Down Pavlova (page 108) and Frozen Fudge Pop Pie (page 95).

2 large egg whites, at room temperature
¼ teaspoon cream of tartar
⅛ teaspoon salt
½ cup sugar
½ teaspoon vanilla extract

Preheat the oven to 225°F. and coat a baking sheet with nonstick cooking spray.

Beat the egg whites with an electric mixer set at high until foamy. Add the cream of tartar and salt and continue beating. Gradually add the sugar and beat until stiff peaks form. Add the vanilla and beat at medium speed just until blended.

Spoon the batter by rounded teaspoonfuls onto the baking sheet, making either 12 large meringues or 24 smaller ones. Bake for 50 to 60 minutes or until the meringues are firm. They will not brown. Cool on a wire rack.

**A**dding a little cocoa powder to meringues adds very few calories and lots of good flavor. Mixing the cocoa with the sugar ensures that it mixes with the meringue lump free.

>    2  large egg whites, at room temperature
>    ¼  teaspoon cream of tartar
>    ⅛  teaspoon salt
>    ½  cup sugar
>    2  tablespoons cocoa powder
>    ½  teaspoon vanilla extract

Preheat the oven to 225°F. and coat a baking sheet with nonstick cooking spray.

Beat the egg whites with an electric mixer set at high until foamy. Add the cream of tartar and salt and continue beating. Gradually add the sugar. When you have added ¼ cup of sugar, mix the remaining ¼ cup with the cocoa. Gradually add the cocoa and sugar mixture to the meringue and beat until stiff peaks form. Add the vanilla and beat at medium speed just until blended.

Spoon the batter by rounded teaspoonfuls onto the baking sheet, making either 12 large meringues or 24 smaller ones. Bake for 50 to 60 minutes or until the meringues are firm. They will not brown. Cool on a wire rack.

# Cocoa Meringues

<u>Yield:</u> 12 large or 24 small meringues

<u>Calories per meringue:</u>
    40 for large meringues; 20 for small meringues

<u>Fat per meringue:</u> 0

<u>Percent of calories from fat:</u> 0

# Divine Almond Macaroons

**Yield:** 12 cookies

**Calories per cookie:** 36

**Fat per cookie:** 1.1 grams

**Percent of calories from fat:** 28%

These delicate meringue cookies have a terrific almond flavor provided by the almond extract and the sliced almonds. The oats give them pleasant bulk and chewiness. Handle the fragile confections carefully—but don't worry about eating more than one. They are practically fat free and have only 36 calories each.

> 1 large egg white, at room temperature
> ¼ teaspoon cream of tartar
> ¼ cup sugar
> ½ teaspoon almond extract
> ½ teaspoon vanilla extract
> 2 tablespoons sliced almonds
> ½ cup old-fashioned rolled oats

Preheat the oven to 350°F. and coat a baking sheet with nonstick cooking spray.

Beat the egg white with an electric mixer set at high until foamy. Add the cream of tartar and continue beating. Gradually add the sugar and beat until stiff peaks form. Add the almond and vanilla extracts and beat at medium speed just until blended. Fold the almonds and oats into the meringue.

Drop the batter by rounded teaspoonfuls onto the baking sheet and bake for 15 minutes or until the cookies are lightly browned. Lift them off the baking sheet very carefully as they are fragile. Cool on a wire rack.

Traditionally, snickerdoodles are short, rich, buttery cookies flavored with cinnamon. These have about half the fat of the original but still pack a wallop of flavor. Just ask our kids! They love them.

½ cup (1 stick) margarine

1¾ cups sugar

2 tablespoons skim milk

1 large egg

2 large egg whites

2¾ cups unbleached all-purpose flour

2 teaspoons cream of tartar

1 teaspoon baking soda

1 teaspoon salt

1 teaspoon ground cinnamon

Preheat the oven to 350°F. and coat 2 baking sheets with nonstick cooking spray.

Beat the margarine and 1½ cups sugar with an electric mixer until fluffy. Add the milk, egg, and egg whites and beat again. Add the flour, cream of tartar, baking soda, and salt and beat until well mixed.

Combine the remaining sugar and the cinnamon in a shallow plate or bowl.

Shape the dough into 1-inch balls and roll them in the cinnamon sugar to coat on all sides. The dough will be sticky. If it's too difficult to handle, flour your hands lightly.

Arrange the balls of dough on the baking sheets and flatten them slightly with your fingers or the back of a spoon. Bake for 8 to 10 minutes or until the cookies are lightly browned. Cool the cookies on the baking sheet for about 5 minutes and then transfer to a wire rack to cool completely. Repeat until all the cookies are baked.

# Snicker-doodles Light

Yield: 72 cookies

Calories per cookie: 32

Fat per cookie: 1.3 grams

Percent of calories from fat: 36%

# Cherry-Almond Biscotti

Yield: 40 cookies

Calories per cookie: 59

Fat per cookie: 1 gram

Percent of calories from fat: 15%

*Biscotti are delightful cookies, very low in fat and calories, and great to have on hand as they keep for a week or more. They also travel well and so are perfect for brown baggers. They take a little effort to form and then must be baked twice to achieve their distinctive crunchy texture. Many people like biscotti for dunking in hot drinks. We like them any which way, especially when chock full of flavorful dried cherries.*

2 large eggs

2 large egg whites

1 cup sugar

2 teaspoons almond extract

2 cups unbleached all-purpose flour

1 teaspoon baking powder

½ teaspoon baking soda

¼ teaspoon salt

1 cup coarsely chopped dried cherries

¼ cup chopped almonds

Preheat the oven to 325°F. and coat a baking sheet with nonstick cooking spray.

Beat the eggs, egg whites, sugar, and almond extract with an electric mixer until smooth. Add the flour, baking powder, baking soda, and salt and beat until well mixed. Stir in the cherries and almonds. The dough will be sticky, but if it seems too sticky, add a few tablespoons of flour.

Drop the dough by large spoonfuls along the baking sheet to form 2 vertical lines. The spoonfuls of dough should be close together (Figure 1). With lightly floured hands, work these 2 lines to make 2 parallel rolls of dough lining each side of the baking sheet (Figure 2). Leave ample room for spreading between the rolls and on the sides of the baking sheet. Each roll will spread during baking so that it is about 5 inches wide.

Bake the rolls for 20 to 25 minutes or until lightly browned and slightly firm to the touch.

Take the rolls from the oven and reduce the temperature to 300°F. Cool the baked rolls of dough on the baking sheet for 10 minutes.

Using a serrated knife, cut each roll into 20 slices. Turn each slice on its side as it's cut (Figure 3).

Bake the biscotti for 10 minutes. Turn the slices onto their other sides and return the baking sheet to the oven for 10 to 20 minutes longer. The biscotti on the ends will be done after 20 minutes total. The rest of the slices may need the full 30 minutes. Watch carefully to avoid overbrowning. Cool the biscotti on wire racks.

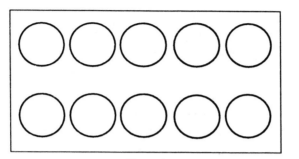

Figure 1.

Figure 2.

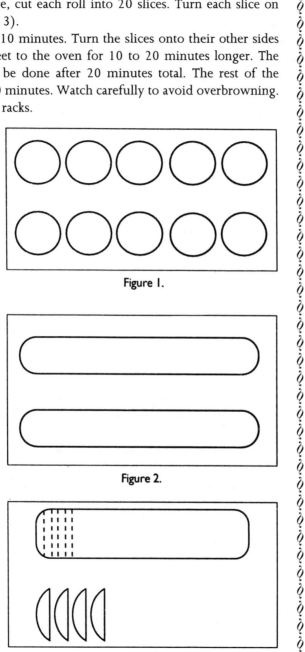

Figure 3.

# Orange Biscotti

**Yield:** 40 cookies

**Calories per cookie:**
44 without apricots; 55 with apricots

**Fat per cookie:**
.4 gram without apricots; .4 gram with apricots

**Percent of calories from fat:**
8% without apricots; 7% with apricots

Try this orange-flavored biscotti. Be sure to grate the colorful part of the orange rind coarsely so that it shows up boldly in the baked cookies. Remember that only the orange part of the rind tastes good; avoid the bitter white pith. We sometimes like to add finely chopped dried apricots for extra flavor and nutrition. The apricots add no more fat but do up the calorie count by 11 per cookie.

2 large eggs

2 large egg whites

1 cup sugar

1 tablespoon orange juice concentrate

1 tablespoon coarsely grated orange rind

1 teaspoon orange extract

2¼ cups unbleached all-purpose flour

1 teaspoon baking powder

½ teaspoon baking soda

¼ teaspoon salt

1 cup finely chopped dried apricots (optional)

Preheat the oven to 325°F. and coat a baking sheet with nonstick cooking spray.

Beat the eggs, egg whites, sugar, orange juice concentrate, orange rind, and orange extract with an electric mixer until smooth. Add the flour, baking powder, baking soda, and salt and beat until well mixed. Stir in the apricots, if using. The dough will be sticky, but if it seems too sticky, add a few tablespoons of flour.

Drop the dough by large spoonfuls along the baking sheet to form 2 vertical lines. The spoonfuls of dough should be close together (Figure 1, page 43). With lightly floured hands, work these 2 lines to make 2 parallel rolls of dough lining each side of the baking sheet (Figure 2). Leave ample room for spreading between the rolls and on the sides of the baking sheet. Each roll will spread during baking so that it is about 5 inches wide.

Bake the rolls for 20 to 25 minutes or until lightly browned and slightly firm to the touch.

Take the rolls from the oven and reduce the temperature to 300°F. Cool the baked rolls of dough on the baking sheet for 10 minutes.

Using a serrated knife, cut each roll into 20 slices. Turn each slice on its side as it's cut (Figure 3, page 43).

Bake the biscotti for 10 minutes. Turn the slices onto their other sides and return the baking sheet to the oven for 10 to 20 minutes longer. The biscotti on the ends will be done after 20 minutes total. The rest of the slices may need the full 30 minutes. Watch carefully to avoid overbrowning. Cool the biscotti on wire racks.

# Ginger Chews

**Yield:** 72 cookies

**Calories per cookie:** 33

**Fat per cookie:** .3 gram

**Percent of calories from fat:** 11%

These little balls, tasting robustly of ginger, have less than a gram of fat and only 33 calories each. Michelle, one of our teenage taste testers, eats a handful of them with a glass of skim milk for "breakfast on the run."

½ cup packed brown sugar

2 tablespoons (¼ stick) margarine

¾ cup molasses

⅓ cup unsweetened apple juice

3 cups unbleached all-purpose flour

1 teaspoon baking soda

1 teaspoon ground ginger

½ teaspoon ground cinnamon

¼ teaspoon salt

Beat the brown sugar, margarine, and molasses with an electric mixer until smooth. Add the apple juice and beat again. Add the flour, baking soda, ginger, cinnamon, and salt and beat until well mixed. Cover and refrigerate for at least 3 hours.

Preheat the oven to 350°F. and coat 2 baking sheets with nonstick cooking spray.

Roll the chilled dough into balls about the size of a large marble. Arrange the balls on the baking sheets and flatten them slightly with your fingers or the back of a spoon. Bake for 10 to 12 minutes or until the cookies are lightly browned. For extra-crisp cookies, bake for an additional minute. Cool the cookies on a wire rack. Repeat until all the cookies are baked.

I t's not easy to make a low-fat cookie with crispy crunch, but because these are baked twice, similar to biscotti, they are delightfully crunchy. They travel well, so think about them for school lunch sacks and weekend hikes.

1 large egg

2 large egg whites

⅓ cup granulated sugar

⅓ cup packed brown sugar

5 tablespoons natural crunchy-style peanut butter

1½ teaspoons vanilla extract

2 cups unbleached all-purpose flour

1 tablespoon baking powder

¼ cup chopped dry-roasted peanuts

Preheat the oven to 350°F. and coat a baking sheet with nonstick cooking spray.

Beat the egg, egg whites, sugars, peanut butter, and vanilla with an electric mixer until smooth. Add the flour and baking powder and beat until well mixed. Stir the peanuts into the dough.

Drop the dough by large spoonfuls along the baking sheet to form 2 vertical lines. The spoonfuls of dough should be close together (Figure 1, page 43). With lightly floured hands, work these 2 lines to make 2 parallel rolls of dough lining each side of the baking sheet (Figure 2). Leave ample room for spreading between the rolls and on the sides of the baking sheet. Each roll will spread during baking so that it is about 5 inches wide.

Bake the rolls for about 20 minutes or until lightly browned and slightly firm to the touch.

Take the rolls from the oven and reduce the temperature to 300°F. Cool the baked rolls of dough on the baking sheet for 10 minutes.

Using a serrated knife, cut each roll into 24 slices. Turn each slice on its side as it's cut (Figure 3, page 43).

Bake the cookies for 10 minutes. Turn the slices onto their other sides and return the baking sheet to the oven for about 5 minutes longer. The cookies on the ends will be done sooner than the rest. Watch carefully to avoid overbrowning. Cool the cookies on wire racks.

# Peanut Butter Crunchies

Yield: 48 cookies

Calories per cookie: 44

Fat per cookie: 1.4 grams

Percent of calories from fat: 29%

47

Cookies

# Fruit 'n Spice Cookies

**Yield:** 48 cookies

**Calories per cookie:** 55

**Fat per cookie:** 1 gram

**Percent of calories from fat:** 16%

*P*runes, raisins, dates, and apricots meet here for a truly delicious, but also healthful sweet.

¼ cup pitted prunes

2 tablespoons very hot (not boiling) orange juice

1 large egg

2 large egg whites

½ cup packed brown sugar

½ cup granulated sugar

¼ cup low-fat cream cheese

2 tablespoons vegetable oil

1 teaspoon vanilla extract

1¾ cups unbleached all-purpose flour

½ teaspoon baking soda

1 teaspoon ground cinnamon

½ teaspoon grated nutmeg

¼ teaspoon salt

½ cup raisins

½ cup chopped dates

¼ cup chopped dried apricots

Preheat the oven to 350°F. and coat 2 baking sheets with nonstick cooking spray.

Soak the prunes in the hot orange juice for about 10 minutes. Puree the prunes and any juice not absorbed by them in a blender until smooth.

Beat the prune puree, egg, egg whites, and sugars with an electric mixer until smooth. Add the cream cheese, oil, and vanilla and beat again.

Toss the flour, baking soda, cinnamon, nutmeg, and salt with the raisins, dates, and apricots. Add this mixture to the batter and mix by hand just until blended.

Divide the dough into 4 sections. Working directly on the baking sheets, roll each piece into a 12-inch log. There will be 2 logs on each sheet. Flatten each log slightly with your fingers or a rubber spatula.

Bake the logs for about 15 minutes or until they have puffed up and are lightly browned. Cool completely on the baking sheets. When cool, cut each log into twelve 1-inch slices.

This classic German-Jewish cookie is similar to biscotti. It's a small, dry cookie great for dunking in coffee, tea, or hot chocolate. Try them with chocolate chips for a little extra panache—the kids love them this way.

2 large eggs
¾ cup sugar
¼ cup vegetable oil
1½ teaspoons vanilla extract
2½ cups unbleached all-purpose flour
1 tablespoon baking powder
½ cup semisweet chocolate chips (optional)

Preheat the oven to 350°F. and coat a baking sheet with nonstick cooking spray.

Beat the eggs, sugar, oil, and vanilla with an electric mixer until smooth. Add the flour and baking powder and beat until well mixed. Stir the chocolate chips into the dough, if using.

Drop the dough by large spoonfuls along the baking sheet to form 2 vertical lines. The spoonfuls of dough should be close together (Figure 1, page 43). With lightly floured hands, work these 2 lines to make 2 parallel rolls of dough lining each side of the baking sheet (Figure 2). Leave ample room for spreading between the rolls and on the sides of the baking sheet. Each roll will spread during baking so that it is about 5 inches wide.

Bake the rolls for about 20 minutes or until lightly browned and slightly firm to the touch.

Take the rolls from the oven and reduce the temperature to 300°F. Cool the baked rolls of dough on the baking sheet for 10 minutes.

Using a serrated knife, cut each roll into 24 slices. Turn each slice on its side as it's cut (Figure 3, page 43).

Bake the cookies for 10 minutes. Turn the slices onto their other sides and return the baking sheet to the oven for about 5 minutes longer. The cookies on the ends will be done sooner than the rest. Watch carefully to avoid overbrowning. Cool the cookies on wire racks.

# Mandelbrot

**Yield:** 48 cookies

**Calories per cookie:**
52 without chocolate chips; 57 with chocolate chips

**Fat per cookie:**
1.5 grams without chocolate chips; 2.2 grams with chocolate chips

**Percent of calories from fat:**
26% without chocolate chips; 35% with chocolate chips

# Dr. Cookie Brownies

**Yield:** 16 brownies

**Calories per brownie:** 85

**Fat per brownie:** 3.5 grams

**Percent of calories from fat:** 37%

**M**ost brownies are prohibitively high in fat. Our solution to this pressing problem was to create a low-fat recipe that does not sacrifice great brownie flavor or fudgy texture. Try them. Chances are you'll agree with our kids that these brownies are "awesome" with a glass of cold skim milk or a bowl of frozen yogurt or ice milk.

2 egg whites

¼ cup vegetable oil

¾ cup packed brown sugar

1 tablespoon nonfat gelatin-free plain yogurt

1 teaspoon vanilla extract

½ cup unbleached all-purpose flour

2 tablespoons cocoa powder

⅛ teaspoon salt

Preheat the oven to 325°F. and coat an 8-inch square pan with nonstick cooking spray.

Beat the egg whites, oil, and brown sugar with an electric mixer until smooth. Add the yogurt and vanilla and beat again. Add the flour, cocoa, and salt and beat until well mixed. Spread the batter in the pan.

Bake for 20 to 25 minutes or until a toothpick inserted in the center of the brownies comes out clean. Cool completely in the pan. When cool, cut into 16 squares. Store the brownies in the refrigerator.

**B**ananas and chocolate are a winning combination and in this recipe, the bananas provide rich moistness as well as flavor. No one will guess these are low fat—but they are! Not even 1 gram per brownie.

1 cup quick-cooking oats (not instant)
1 cup boiling water
4 large egg whites
¾ cup packed brown sugar
½ cup granulated sugar
2 tablespoons vegetable oil
1 teaspoon vanilla extract
1½ cups mashed ripe bananas (about 3 bananas)
1 cup unbleached all-purpose flour
1 teaspoon baking soda
½ teaspoon salt
4 tablespoons cocoa powder

Preheat the oven to 350°F. and coat a 9-by-13-inch pan with nonstick cooking spray.

Mix the oats with the boiling water and set aside for about 5 minutes or until the water is absorbed by the oats.

Beat the egg whites, sugars, oil, vanilla, and bananas with an electric mixer until smooth. Add the flour, baking soda, salt, cocoa, and soaked oats and beat until well mixed. Spread the batter in the pan.

Bake for 20 to 25 minutes or until a toothpick inserted in the center of the brownies comes out clean. Cool completely in the pan. When cool, cut into 48 squares. (These brownies are much easier to cut if you put the cooled brownies, in the pan, in the freezer for about 20 minutes.) Store the brownies in the refrigerator.

# Chocolate Banana Brownies

**Yield:** 48 brownies

**Calories per brownie:** 50

**Fat per brownie:** .8 gram

**Percent of calories from fat:** 14%

# Fruitcake Brownies

**Yield:** 16 brownies

**Calories per brownie:** 100

**Fat per brownie:** 1.9 grams

**Percent of calories from fat:** 17%

If you like fruitcake, you'll love these fruity, nutty bars. And it's no mistake: we did not forget the oil; we left it out! Instead, we splurged on nuts. Mixed, candied fruits are sometimes sold as "fruitcake mix."

1 large egg

¾ cup packed brown sugar

1 teaspoon vanilla extract

¾ cup unbleached all-purpose flour

¼ teaspoon baking soda

¼ teaspoon salt

⅓ cup mixed candied fruit, chopped into ¼-inch pieces if not already chopped

⅓ cup raisins

⅓ cup chopped walnuts, pecans, or almonds

Preheat the oven to 350°F. and coat an 8-inch square pan with nonstick cooking spray.

Beat the egg, brown sugar, and vanilla with an electric mixer until smooth. Add the flour, baking soda, and salt and beat until well mixed. Stir the fruit and nuts into the batter. The batter will be very thick. Spread the batter in the pan.

Bake for 20 to 25 minutes or until the brownies puff up and a toothpick inserted in the center comes out clean. Cool completely in the pan. When cool, cut into 16 squares.

$W$ho hasn't joked about prunes now and again? But the fact is, they are terrific for regularity, and when eaten whole, they supply a good amount of soluble dietary fiber. Most gratifying is how moist and sweet they make these bar cookies, especially when mixed with chopped apples.

1 large egg

¾ cup packed brown sugar

2 tablespoons vegetable oil

1 teaspoon vanilla extract

½ cup chopped pitted prunes

1 cup unbleached all-purpose flour

1 teaspoon baking powder

¼ teaspoon salt

½ cup chopped unpeeled apple (1 small apple, or less)

Preheat the oven to 350°F. and coat an 8-inch square pan with nonstick cooking spray.

Beat the egg, brown sugar, oil, and vanilla in an electric mixer until smooth.

Toss the prunes with the flour to keep them from sticking together. Stir the prunes, flour, baking powder, salt, and chopped apple into the batter by hand. Spread the batter in the pan.

Bake for about 30 minutes or until a toothpick inserted in the center of the pan comes out clean. Cool in the pan and then cut into 16 squares. Store in the refrigerator.

# Apple-Prune Squares

**Yield:** 16 bar cookies

**Calories per bar:** 97

**Fat per bar:** 2 grams

**Percent of calories from fat:** 19%

# Chocolate Date Squares

**Yield:** 16 bar cookies

**Calories per bar:** 137

**Fat per bar:** 3.4 grams

**Percent of calories from fat:** 22%

**D**ates, the fruit of the towering date palm tree, are desert fare that go down very well for dessert. They are widely used in the Middle East, where they grow naturally. They are also quite popular in the United States, where they are grown in the arid regions of California and Arizona. Dates add marvelous moistness and a lush, sweet flavor to baked goods—particularly when mixed with chocolate chips. Be sure the dates you buy are moist and plump, not hard and dry.

2 large egg whites

¾ cup packed brown sugar

3 tablespoons vegetable oil

¼ cup natural unsweetened applesauce

1 teaspoon vanilla extract

1¼ cups unbleached all-purpose flour

1¼ teaspoons baking powder

⅛ teaspoon salt

1 cup chopped dates

¼ cup semisweet chocolate chips

Preheat the oven to 350°F. and coat an 8-inch square pan with nonstick cooking spray.

Beat the egg whites, brown sugar, and oil with an electric mixer until smooth. Add the applesauce and vanilla and beat again. Add the flour, baking powder, and salt and beat until well mixed. Stir the dates and chocolate chips into the batter. Spread the batter in the pan.

Bake for about 25 minutes or until a toothpick inserted in the center of the pan comes out clean. Cool in the pan and then cut into 16 squares. Store in the refrigerator.

*What we love about these squares is that they provide excellent fiber—the oats and the oat bran—as well as great flavor. Our kids grab them when they don't have time for a sit-down breakfast, and the whole family snacks on them when we need some quick energy.*

1 large egg white

¼ cup honey

¼ cup natural creamy-style peanut butter

½ teaspoon vanilla extract

1¼ cups old-fashioned rolled oats

¼ cup oat bran

¼ teaspoon ground cinnamon

½ cup raisins

Preheat the oven to 350°F. and coat an 8-inch square pan with nonstick cooking spray.

Beat the egg white, honey, peanut butter, and vanilla with an electric mixer until smooth. Add the oats, bran, and cinnamon and beat until well mixed. Stir the raisins into the batter. Spread the batter in the pan.

Bake for about 20 minutes or until a toothpick inserted in the center of the pan comes out clean. Cool in the pan and then cut into 16 squares. Store in the refrigerator.

# Peanut Butter and Honey Breakfast Squares

**Yield:** 16 bar cookies

**Calories per bar:** 82

**Fat per bar:** 2 grams

**Percent of calories from fat:** 22%

# Dr. Cookie Peanut Butter Squares

**Yield:** 16 bar cookies

**Calories per bar:** 89

**Fat per bar:** 2.8 grams

**Percent of calories from fat:** 28%

*You have a choice: Do you like intense peanutty flavor? Or do you prefer a little chocolate mixed with your peanuts? Choose either dry-roasted peanuts in these luscious bar cookies or a handful of mini chocolate chips (the larger chips work fine if that is all you have!). Either way, they're spectacular and have just over 2 grams of fat and an equal number of calories.*

¼ cup natural creamy-style peanut butter

¾ cup packed brown sugar

2 large egg whites

½ teaspoon vanilla extract

¾ cup unbleached all-purpose flour

1 teaspoon baking powder

2 tablespoons chopped dry-roasted peanuts or semisweet mini chocolate chips

Preheat the oven to 350°F. and coat an 8-inch square pan with nonstick cooking spray.

Beat the peanut butter and brown sugar with an electric mixer until smooth. Add the egg whites and vanilla and beat again. Add the flour and baking powder and beat until well mixed. Stir the peanuts or chocolate chips into the batter. Spread the batter in the pan.

Bake for about 25 minutes or until a toothpick inserted in the center of the pan comes out clean. Cool in the pan and then cut into 16 squares. Store in the refrigerator.

We make no claims to inventing this all-American treat. But we include it here because it is naturally low in fat and calories and may inspire you to examine some other all-time favorites—they, too, may be low in fat. Wouldn't that be great?

3 tablespoons margarine

10 ounces mini marshmallows

6 cups crisp rice cereal

Coat a 9-by-13-inch baking pan with nonstick cooking spray.

Melt the margarine in a large saucepan. Stir in the marshmallows and melt over medium heat, stirring constantly. Remove the saucepan from the heat and stir in the cereal. Spread the mixture in the baking pan. Cool completely in the pan. Cut into 24 squares.

# Crisp Rice Cereal Treats

**Yield:** 28 bar cookies

**Calories per bar:** 75

**Fat per bar:** 1.5 grams

**Percent of calories from fat:** 18%

# Chapter 2

# Cakes

We begin this chapter with cheesecake. *Cheesecake* in a healthful, low-fat, reduced-calorie dessert and baking book? Hey, Docs, get real, you say. And you're right. Cheesecake does not belong in a book such as this. But we include it to make a very important point: It's okay to indulge every now and then. Some culinary creations—cheesecake being one of them—cannot be improved upon, modified, or otherwise tampered with without destroying the integrity of the original. We say, why fool with perfection?

Just don't eat that perfection every day. Or even every week. But once in a while is not only acceptable, it's beneficial to the soul.

However, you can have your cake and eat it too by following the other fourteen recipes in this chapter. As you may have guessed, we use a lot of fruit, relying on the natural moistness and sweetness of apples and bananas. We count on carrots, pumpkin, and zucchini for similar results. What's more, because we are constitutionally unable to neglect chocolate (it's just too darn good!), we have two recipes for dark, delicious, sinfully indulgent chocolate cakes. One is even called Decadence (page 76).

We make many cakes with some whole wheat flour, oats, and bran for the complex carbohydrates and fiber. We also leave the peel on the apple for the fiber and rich supply of vitamins in the skin. One of our fruit cakes (Marv's Favorite, page 72) is completely fat free; another cake is made with pinto beans, which are a good source of fiber.

After trying a few of the recipes you'll understand why Dr. Cookie says, without apology, "Let everyone eat cake!"

Believe us. We've tried to make a low-fat cheesecake but as far as we're concerned, it just can't be done. We tried cottage cheese, ricotta, yogurt, and quark; we even tried tofu. No dice. They tasted okay, but they still tasted like diet desserts. And that's not our goal. Our conclusion? Life's too short to go without cheesecake—the real thing, that is—and so we have come up with a way for you to get only half the calories and half the fat. Just follow this recipe.

1 slice of your absolute favorite cheesecake
1 very special friend
2 forks

Combine the ingredients. Savor every bite. Talk about how wonderful it is to enjoy great food with even greater friends. Smile a lot. And don't feel guilty.

# Dr. Cookie's World Famous Cheesecake

**Yield:** 2 servings

**Calories per serving:** maybe a zillion

**Fat per serving:** lots of grams

**Percent of calories from fat:** you don't want to know

# Apple-Bran Snack Cake

Yield: 12 servings

Calories per serving: 184

Fat per serving: .9 gram

Percent of calories from fat: 4%

*T*his snack cake is so chock full of good things and so filling we cut it into small pieces. Be sure to leave the apple skins on the apples to get the full benefit of fiber and vitamins. And don't worry if the batter resembles soggy cereal with some apples stirred into it. The appearance and texture improve significantly in the oven.

1½ cups unbleached all-purpose flour

2 teaspoons baking powder

2 teaspoons pumpkin pie spice

¼ teaspoon salt

1½ cups shredded unpeeled apple (about 1 large apple)

2 cups thinly sliced unpeeled apple (about 1 large apple)

½ cup unsweetened apple juice

¼ cup granulated sugar

1 large egg

1 large egg white

½ cup packed brown sugar

2 cups raisin bran or bran flake cereal

Preheat the oven to 350°F. Coat an 8-inch square pan with nonstick cooking spray and dust it lightly with flour. Tap out the excess flour.

Whisk the flour with the baking powder, pie spice, and salt. Set aside.

Toss the grated apple, apple slices, apple juice, and granulated sugar together in a bowl.

In another bowl, beat the egg, egg white, and brown sugar with an electric mixer until smooth. Stir the apple mixture into the batter by hand. Add the flour and stir again. Finally, stir in the cereal. The batter is thick.

Scrape the batter into the pan and bake for 35 to 40 minutes or until a toothpick inserted near the center comes out clean. Cool the cake in the pan set on a wire rack. Cut when completely cool. Store the cake in the pan.

Unsweetened pumpkin puree is a great ingredient that is always easy to find in the markets. We use it here for its moistness and flavor, and add orange juice concentrate for natural sweetness and a good dose of vitamin C.

1⅔ cups unbleached all-purpose flour

1 teaspoon baking powder

½ teaspoon baking soda

½ teaspoon ground cinnamon

½ teaspoon ground allspice

½ teaspoon grated nutmeg

½ teaspoon ground cloves

1 large egg

2 large egg whites

⅔ cup packed brown sugar

¾ cup granulated sugar

3 tablespoons vegetable oil

⅓ cup orange juice concentrate

1 cup unsweetened pumpkin puree

⅔ cup golden raisins

Preheat the oven to 350°F. Coat a 9-by-13-inch pan with nonstick cooking spray and dust it lightly with flour. Tap out the excess flour.

Whisk the flour with the baking powder, baking soda, cinnamon, allspice, nutmeg, and cloves. Set aside.

Beat the egg, egg whites, sugars, and oil with an electric mixer until smooth. Add the concentrate and pumpkin and beat again. Add the flour mixture and beat until well mixed. Stir the raisins into the batter.

Scrape the batter into the pan and bake for 25 to 30 minutes or until a toothpick inserted near the center comes out clean. Cool the cake in the pan set on a wire rack. Cut when completely cool. Store the cake in the pan in the refrigerator.

# Pumpkin Cake Squares

Yield: 15 servings

Calories per serving: 187

Fat per serving: 4.3 grams

Percent of calories from fat: 21%

# Apple-Cranberry Cake

Yield: 12 servings

Calories per serving: 187

Fat per serving: 4.4 grams

Percent of calories from fat: 21%

This is a wonderful cake to make in the fall when the apples are crisp and crunchy and the markets are well stocked with fresh cranberries. It's good, too, other times of year, and you can always substitute raisins or dried cranberries for fresh or frozen cranberries.

2¼ cups unbleached all-purpose flour

1 teaspoon baking soda

1 teaspoon ground cinnamon

¼ teaspoon salt

1 large egg

2 large egg whites

¾ cup sugar

3 tablespoons vegetable oil

¾ cup natural unsweetened applesauce

¾ cup buttermilk

1 cup finely chopped unpeeled apple (about 1 large apple)

1½ cups fresh or frozen and thawed cranberries

Preheat the oven to 350°F. Coat an 8- or 9-inch Bundt pan with nonstick cooking spray and dust it lightly with flour. Tap out the excess flour.

Whisk the flour with the baking soda, cinnamon, and salt. Set aside.

Beat the egg, egg whites, sugar, and oil with an electric mixer until smooth. Add the applesauce and buttermilk and beat again. Add the flour mixture and beat until well mixed. Stir the chopped apple and cranberries into the batter.

Scrape the batter into the pan and bake for 40 to 45 minutes or until a toothpick inserted near the center comes out clean. Cool in the pan for 10 minutes. Carefully remove the cake from the pan and cool completely on a wire rack.

In desert regions where dates are grown, they often are an important source of carbohydrates because, when partly dried, they are about 70 percent sugar. Although we don't need them for the simple carbohydrates, we relish their natural sweetness—especially when teamed with tart cranberries. Look for plump, sticky, moist dates. The fluted pan and generous amount of bright red cranberries make this a particularly attractive cake.

# Cranberry-Date Cake

Yield: 12 servings

Calories per serving:
    224 without walnuts; 256 with walnuts

Fat per serving:
    4.7 grams without walnuts; 7.7 grams with walnuts

Percent of calories from fat:
    27% without walnuts; 19% with walnuts

    2¼ cups unbleached all-purpose flour
    1 teaspoon baking soda
    ¼ teaspoon salt
    1 large egg
    2 large egg whites
    ¾ cup sugar
    3 tablespoons vegetable oil
    1 tablespoon coarsely grated orange rind
    1½ cups buttermilk
    1½ cups fresh or frozen and thawed cranberries
    1 cup chopped dates
    ½ cup chopped walnuts (optional)

Preheat the oven to 350°F. Coat an 8- or 9-inch Bundt pan with nonstick cooking spray and dust it lightly with flour. Tap out the excess flour.

Whisk the flour with the baking soda and salt. Set aside.

Beat the egg, egg whites, sugar, and oil with an electric mixer until smooth. Add the orange rind and buttermilk and beat again. Add the flour mixture and beat until well mixed. Stir the cranberries, dates, and walnuts into the batter.

Scrape the batter into the pan and bake for 40 to 45 minutes or until a toothpick inserted near the center comes out clean. Cool in the pan for 10 minutes. Carefully remove the cake from the pan and cool completely on a wire rack.

# Carrot Cake

Yield: 15 servings

Calories per serving:
219 without frosting; 286 with Nonfat Cream Cheese Frosting; 308 with Cream Cheese Frosting

Fat per serving:
4.7 grams without frosting; 4.7 grams with Nonfat Cream Cheese Frosting; 7.9 grams with Cream Cheese Frosting

Percent of calories from fat:
19% without frosting; 20% with Nonfat Cream Cheese Frosting; 23% with Cream Cheese Frosting

We were, quite frankly, somewhat appalled when we analyzed the carrot cake recipe that we had been making for years: There were 545 calories and 34 grams of fat in every 3-inch piece. And that was before slathering it with rich cream cheese frosting! Our solution? Create a lower-fat, lower-calorie version. We set to work and were absolutely thrilled with the results. We like this cake better than the high-fat one because it's packed with luscious fruit and lots of moist carrots, and it is a lot easier on the conscience and waistline. Try it with or without frosting—and choose either frosting depending on your frame of mind and how much fat you want to allow yourself.

1¾ cups unbleached all-purpose flour

⅔ cup whole wheat flour

2 teaspoons baking soda

2 teaspoons ground cinnamon

1 teaspoon grated nutmeg

¼ teaspoon salt

1 large egg

2 large egg whites

1¼ cups packed brown sugar

¼ cup vegetable oil

3 cups shredded unpeeled carrots (about 4 to 6 carrots)

⅔ cup buttermilk

1 cup unsweetened crushed pineapple, drained

¾ cup raisins

## Nonfat Cream Cheese Frosting

1 8-ounce package nonfat cream cheese

2 cups confectioners' sugar

1 teaspoon vanilla extract

## Cream Cheese Frosting

> 1  8-ounce package Neufchâtel cheese
>
> 2  cups confectioners' sugar
>
> 1  teaspoon vanilla extract
>
> 1  tablespoon skim milk, approximately

Preheat the oven to 350°F. Coat a 9-by-13-inch pan with nonstick cooking spray and dust lightly with flour. Tap out the excess flour.

Whisk the flours with the baking soda, cinnamon, nutmeg, and salt. Set aside.

Beat the egg, egg whites, brown sugar, and oil with an electric mixer until smooth. Add the carrots and beat for 1 minute. Add the buttermilk, pineapple, and raisins and beat again. Add the flour mixture and beat until well mixed.

Scrape the batter into the pan and bake for 30 to 35 minutes or until a toothpick inserted near the center comes out clean. Cool the cake in the pan set on a wire rack. Frost, if desired, when completely cool. Store the cake in the pan in the refrigerator.

To make the Nonfat Cream Cheese Frosting, beat the cream cheese, confectioners' sugar, and vanilla with an electric mixer set at medium-low until the frosting is soft and thin. Alternatively, mix the ingredients by hand with a fork or whisk. When you are ready to serve the cake, spoon the frosting over individual slices after they have been cut.

To make the Cream Cheese Frosting, beat the cheese, confectioners' sugar, and vanilla with an electric mixer set at medium-high until smooth. Reduce the speed to medium-low and add the milk, a teaspoon at a time, until the frosting is at spreading consistency. Spread the frosting on the cooled, uncut cake.

# Carrot-Apple Cake

**Yield:** 15 servings

**Calories per serving:**
210 without frosting;
303 with frosting

**Fat per serving:**
4.6 grams without frosting;
7.8 grams with frosting

**Percent of calories from fat:**
20% without frosting;
23% with frosting

Adding moist, nutritionally rich fruits and vegetables to cake batters is a wonderful way to create low-fat, healthful, and delicious desserts. We like to play with the carrot cake motif and re-create it. Here we add shredded apple and applesauce, and could have named this "apple-carrot cake" just as easily as the reverse.

1½ cups unbleached all-purpose flour
1 cup quick-cooking oats (not instant)
2 teaspoons baking soda
2 teaspoons ground cinnamon
1 teaspoon grated nutmeg
¼ teaspoon salt
1 large egg
1 large egg white
¾ cup packed brown sugar
½ cup granulated sugar
¼ cup vegetable oil
1 cup natural unsweetened applesauce
3 cups shredded unpeeled carrots (about 4 to 6 carrots)
1 cup shredded unpeeled apple (1 large apple)
¾ cup raisins

## Orange Cream Cheese Frosting

1 8-ounce package Neufchâtel cheese
2 cups confectioners' sugar
1 tablespoon orange juice concentrate, approximately

Preheat the oven to 350°F. Coat a 9-by-13-inch pan with nonstick cooking spray and dust lightly with flour. Tap out the excess flour.

Whisk the flour with the oats, baking soda, cinnamon, nutmeg, and salt. Set aside.

Beat the egg, egg white, sugars, and oil with an electric mixer until smooth. Add the applesauce and carrot and beat for 1 minute. Add the flour mixture and beat until well mixed. Stir the apple and raisins into the batter.

Scrape the batter into the pan and bake for 30 to 35 minutes or until a toothpick inserted near the center comes out clean. Cool the cake in the pan set on a wire rack. Frost, if desired, when completely cool. Store the cake in the pan in the refrigerator.

To make the Orange Cream Cheese Frosting, beat the cheese, confectioners' sugar, and orange juice concentrate with an electric mixer set at medium-low until the frosting is smooth and soft enough to spread over the cake. Add more concentrate if necessary. Alternatively, mix the ingredients by hand with a fork or whisk. Spread the frosting on the cooled, uncut cake.

# Banana-Carrot Cake

**Yield:** 9 servings

**Calories per serving:**
    252 without walnuts;
    273 with walnuts

**Fat per serving:**
    4 grams without walnuts;
    6 grams with walnuts

**Percent of calories from fat:**
    14% without walnuts;
    20% with walnuts

In this recipe, we combined shredded carrots with ripe bananas for even more moistness and natural sweetness. This dynamic duo provides a good amount of potassium, beta-carotene (vitamin A), and iron.

1½ cups unbleached all-purpose flour

1 teaspoon baking soda

½ teaspoon ground cinnamon

½ teaspoon grated nutmeg

1 large egg

½ cup packed brown sugar

½ cup granulated sugar

2 tablespoons vegetable oil

1½ cups mashed ripe bananas (about 3 bananas)

1 cup shredded unpeeled carrots (about 1 to 2 carrots)

½ cup raisins

¼ cup chopped walnuts (optional)

Preheat the oven to 350°F. Coat an 8-inch square pan with nonstick cooking spray and dust it lightly with flour. Tap out the excess flour.

Whisk the flour with the baking soda, cinnamon, and nutmeg. Set aside.

Beat the egg, sugars, and oil with an electric mixer until smooth. Add the bananas and carrots and beat again. Add the flour mixture, raisins, and walnuts and beat until well mixed.

Scrape the batter into the pan and bake for 40 to 45 minutes or until a toothpick inserted near the center comes out clean. Cool the cake in the pan set on a wire rack. Cut when completely cool. Store the cake in the pan in the refrigerator.

This filling cake is as good for breakfast as it is for dessert or a mid-afternoon snack. We make it with whatever fruit is in season and ripe at the time, sometimes combining two or three different kinds or using, perhaps, only ripe, juicy peaches from a nearby orchard. If you lay the fruit on top of the batter rather than stirring it into the batter, you can make pretty patterns.

- 1 cup old-fashioned rolled oats
- 1¾ cups boiling water
- 1¾ cups unbleached all-purpose flour
- 1 teaspoon baking soda
- 1 teaspoon ground cinnamon
- ¼ teaspoon grated nutmeg
- ¼ teaspoon salt
- 1 large egg
- 2 large egg whites
- 1 cup packed brown sugar
- ½ cup honey
- 3 tablespoons vegetable oil
- 2 cups sliced, fresh plums, peaches, apples, blueberries, or any other fresh fruit

Preheat the oven to 350°F. Coat a 9-by-13-inch pan with nonstick cooking spray and dust it lightly with flour. Tap out the excess flour.

Stir the oats into the boiling water and set aside until cooled to lukewarm.

Whisk the flour with the baking soda, cinnamon, nutmeg, and salt. Set aside.

Beat the egg, egg whites, brown sugar, honey, and oil with an electric mixer until smooth. Add the oats and beat for 1 minute. Add the flour mixture and beat until just mixed. Stir the fruit into the batter. Alternatively, arrange the fruit on top of the batter after it is in the pan.

Scrape the batter into the pan and bake for 35 to 40 minutes or until a toothpick inserted near the center comes out clean. Cool the cake in the pan set on a wire rack. Cut when completely cool. Store the cake in the pan.

# Oatmeal Fresh Fruit Cake

Yield: 15 servings

Calories per serving: 192

Fat per serving: 3 grams

Percent of calories from fat: 14%

# Marv's Favorite Fruitcake

**Yield:** 14 servings

**Calories per serving:** 157

**Fat per serving:** 0

**Percent of calories from fat:** 0

*How about this? A fat-free cake! We added lots of fruit to compensate for the lack of fat and sweetened the cake with brown sugar and honey so that it is as moist, lovely, and wonderful as a light, modern fruitcake should be. You can usually buy dried fruits at the supermarket, but if not, try the natural foods store.*

½ cup raisins

½ cup golden raisins

½ cup chopped pitted prunes

1 cup chopped mixed natural fruit, such as dried pears, apples, apricots, and pineapple

1 cup plus 2 tablespoons unbleached all-purpose flour

½ teaspoon baking powder

¼ teaspoon grated nutmeg

¼ teaspoon ground cardamom

¼ teaspoon salt

4 egg whites

½ cup packed brown sugar

¾ cup natural unsweetened applesauce

3 tablespoons honey

1 tablespoon coarsley chopped orange peel

1 teaspoon vanilla extract

Preheat the oven to 300°F. Coat a 9-by-5-inch loaf pan with nonstick cooking spray and line the pan with aluminum foil. Coat the foil with nonstick cooking spray.

Toss the raisins, prunes, and other fruit with 2 tablespoons of the flour. Set aside.

Whisk the remaining 1 cup flour with the baking powder, nutmeg, cardamom, and salt. Set aside.

Beat the egg whites and brown sugar with an electric mixer until smooth. Add the applesauce, honey, orange peel, and vanilla and beat again. Add the flour mixture and beat until well mixed. Fold the fruit into the batter.

Scrape the batter into the pan and bake for about 1 hour and 35 to

45 minutes or until the cake is lightly browned and a toothpick inserted near the center comes out clean. Check the cake about every 10 minutes after the first hour to make sure it is not browning too much. If so, shield it with a piece of foil over the top of the pan. Cool the cake in the pan set on a wire rack for 15 minutes. Invert the pan and carefully remove the cake, peeling off the foil and setting it upright on the rack to cool completely. Store the cake in the refrigerator.

# Surprise Cake

Yield: 12 servings

Calories per serving:
202 without glaze; 214 with glaze

Fat per serving:
4 grams without glaze; 4 grams
with glaze

Percent of calories from fat:
18% without glaze; 17% with
glaze

**W**e spend nearly every day of our lives in hospitals and, believe it or not, we don't complain about hospital food! We've met some incredibly dedicated hospital cooks and dieticians who, with the stroke of a whisk, debunk the common myth that hospital food is horrid. For instance, this recipe was developed by a hospital dietician who works very hard to please the patients and staff—and always succeeds. We call it "Surprise Cake" because the guest ingredient is canned pinto or kidney beans. They add great texture and moisture, plus they are a good source of fiber. For fun, tint the glaze pink with red food coloring and decorate the cake with those jelly beans that resemble kidney beans.

    1 cup unbleached all-purpose flour

    1 teaspoon baking soda

    2 teaspoons ground cinnamon

    1 teaspoon ground cloves

    ½ teaspoon ground allspice

    ¼ teaspoon salt

    1 large egg

    1 large egg white

    ¾ cup sugar

    3 tablespoons vegetable oil

    2 cups cooked and mashed pinto or kidney beans

    1 teaspoon vanilla extract

    1 cup finely chopped unpeeled apple (about 1 apple)

    1 cup raisins

## Optional glaze

    ¼ cup confectioners' sugar

    2 teaspoons orange juice

Preheat the oven to 350°F. Coat an 8- or 9-inch Bundt pan with nonstick cooking spray and dust it lightly with flour. Tap out the excess flour.

Whisk the flour with the baking soda, cinnamon, cloves, allspice, and salt. Set aside.

Beat the egg, egg white, sugar, and oil with an electric mixer until smooth. Add the beans and vanilla and beat again. Add the flour mixture and beat until well mixed. Stir the chopped apple and raisins into the batter.

Scrape the batter into the pan and bake for 35 to 40 minutes or until a toothpick inserted near the center comes out clean. Cool in the pan for 10 minutes. Carefully remove the cake from the pan and cool completely on a wire rack.

To glaze, whisk the confectioners' sugar with the orange juice until smooth. Drizzle the glaze over the cooled cake.

# Chocolate Decadence with Raspberry Sauce

Yield: 8 servings

Calories per serving: 184

Fat per serving: 6 grams

Percent of calories from fat: 30%

Who said it couldn't be done? At first even we weren't sure we could create a sumptuous, sinful chocolate cake that would fit the criteria for the book. Happily, we dispelled our own doubt. This cake is a splendid example of what chocolate lovers with a lot of perseverance can accomplish. And believe us, this is a cake for chocolate lovers. Serve it without the raspberry sauce, if you prefer, and keep in mind that the cake actually gets fudgier when stored in the refrigerator for a day. It's also good after freezing. (Hint: Keep a cake in the freezer for those times you have a serious chocolate craving.) Use the raspberry sauce for topping other desserts such as Peach Melba (page 101).

½ cup old-fashioned rolled oats

¾ cup boiling water

½ cup unbleached all-purpose flour

½ teaspoon baking soda

¼ teaspoon salt

¼ cup cocoa powder

½ cup granulated sugar

¼ cup packed brown sugar

3 tablespoons vegetable oil

½ teaspoon vanilla extract

2 large egg whites

¼ cup semisweet chocolate chips

Fresh raspberries, for garnish (optional)

## Raspberry Sauce

1 pint fresh or frozen and thawed raspberries

1½ teaspoons cornstarch

1 tablespoon cold water

3 tablespoons confectioners' sugar

Preheat the oven to 350°F. Coat an 8-inch round cake pan with nonstick cooking spray.

Stir the oats into the boiling water and set aside until cooled to luke-warm.

Whisk the flour with the baking soda, salt, and cocoa in the bowl of the electric mixer. Do not turn on the mixer.

Add the oats, sugars, oil, and vanilla and beat for 2 minutes. Add the egg whites and beat for 2 more minutes.

Scrape the batter into the pan and sprinkle the top with chocolate chips. Bake for about 30 minutes or until a toothpick inserted near the center of the cake comes out clean. Cool the cake in the pan for about 5 minutes and then turn out on a wire rack to cool completely. Serve the cake on a beautiful plate, garnished with raspberries if desired, and pass the raspberry sauce at the table for spooning over each slice.

To make the Raspberry Sauce, process the berries in a food processor or blender until smooth. If fresh berries appear dry, add 3 tablespoons water; if using frozen berries, include any liquid. Press the puree through a wire sieve to remove the seeds.

Mix the cornstarch with the cold water to make a smooth paste. Mix the seedless puree with the sugar in a small, heavy saucepan. Bring to a boil, then add the cornstarch paste and boil for 1 minute, stirring constantly. Remove the sauce from the heat, cool, and store in the refrigerator until ready to use.

# Chocolate Pudding Cake

Yield: 9 servings

Calories per serving: 171

Fat per serving: 3 grams

Percent of calories from fat: 16%

We updated this old-fashioned comfort dessert for the 1990s. We took away some of the fat and calories but left all the warm, soft, gooey chocolate. The hot liquid poured over the cake batter just before baking turns into a lovely chocolaty sauce that mingles with the cake when it is cut. If you like the flavor of mocha, use coffee; otherwise use hot water. Serve this warm or cold (we prefer it warm), with or without nonfat vanilla frozen yogurt.

⅓ cup packed brown sugar

¼ cup plus 2 tablespoons cocoa powder

1 cup unbleached all-purpose flour

⅔ cup granulated sugar

2 teaspoons baking powder

¼ teaspoon salt

½ cup skim milk

2 tablespoons (¼ stick) margarine, melted

1 teaspoon vanilla extract

1⅓ cups very hot brewed coffee or very hot (not boiling) water

Preheat the oven to 350°F. Coat an 8-inch square pan with nonstick cooking spray.

Mix the brown sugar and 2 tablespoons cocoa with a fork until the mixture is lump free. Set aside.

Whisk the flour with the remaining ¼ cup cocoa, granulated sugar, baking powder, and salt. Set aside.

Beat the milk, margarine, and vanilla with an electric mixer until smooth. Add the flour mixture and beat until well mixed.

Scrape the batter into the pan and sprinkle the top with the brown sugar mixture. Pour the coffee or hot water over the batter. Bake for 25 to 30 minutes or until the top looks browned and firm. The bottom of the cake will stay soft and puddinglike. Cool for 10 minutes in the pan and then serve directly from the pan. Store the cake in the pan in the refrigerator.

Zucchini has a tendency to take over the garden come September and if your family is like ours, they probably get a little tired of the vegetable. We invented this cake expressly for the annual zucchini invasion. We have other recipes for zucchini scattered throughout the book, and we hope all will help use up the abundant crop deliciously and expediently. If not, let the zucchs grow to outrageous proportions and use them for doorstops or dress them up as zucchini monsters for Halloween.

1 cup unbleached all-purpose flour
1 cup whole wheat flour
1 teaspoon baking powder
1 teaspoon ground cinnamon
¼ teaspoon salt
2 large eggs
2 large egg whites
⅔ cup packed brown sugar
¼ cup vegetable oil
1 cup raisins
2 cups shredded zucchini (about 2 to 3 medium zucchini)

Preheat the oven to 350°F. Coat a 9-by-13-inch pan with nonstick cooking spray and dust it lightly with flour. Tap out the excess flour.

Whisk the flours with the baking powder, cinnamon, and salt. Set aside.

Beat the eggs, egg whites, brown sugar, and oil with an electric mixer until smooth. Add the flour mixture and beat until well mixed. Stir the raisins and zucchini into the batter.

Scrape the batter into the pan and bake for 35 to 40 minutes or until a toothpick inserted near the center comes out clean. Cool the cake in the pan set on a wire rack. Cut when completely cool. Store the cake in the pan in the refrigerator.

# Whole Wheat Zucchini Cake

Yield: 15 servings

Calories per serving: 208

Fat per serving: 4.6 grams

Percent of calories from fat: 20%

# Blueberry Cake

**Yield:** 12 servings

**Calories per serving:**
188 without glaze; 200 with glaze

**Fat per serving:**
4 grams without glaze; 4 grams with glaze

**Percent of calories from fat:**
19% without glaze; 18% with glaze

*Some people claim blueberries cure colds; others say they cure diarrhea. We say these claims may have credibility, but our main concern is how wonderful blueberries taste in baked goods. Eating a piece of the cake is one of the best ways we know to get the day off to a great start (serve as you would a coffee cake) or to end the same day on a sweet note.*

2 cups unbleached all-purpose flour

1 teaspoon baking soda

1 teaspoon ground cinnamon

½ teaspoon ground cloves

¼ teaspoon salt

1 large egg

1 large egg white

½ cup sugar

3 tablespoons vegetable oil

1 teaspoon coarsely chopped orange peel

½ cup orange juice

⅓ cup honey

1 teaspoon vanilla extract

1½ cups fresh or frozen and thawed blueberries

## Optional glaze

¼ cup confectioners' sugar

2 teaspoons orange juice

Preheat the oven to 350°F. Coat an 8- or 9-inch Bundt pan with nonstick cooking spray and dust it lightly with flour. Tap out the excess flour.

Whisk the flour with the baking soda, cinnamon, cloves, and salt. Set aside.

Beat the egg, egg white, sugar, and oil with an electric mixer until smooth. Add the orange peel, orange juice, honey, and vanilla and beat again. Add the flour mixture and beat until well mixed. Stir the blueberries gently into the batter.

Scrape the batter into the pan and bake for 35 to 40 minutes or until a toothpick inserted near the center comes out clean. Cool in the pan for 10 minutes. Carefully remove the cake from the pan and cool completely on a wire rack.

To glaze, whisk the confectioners' sugar with the orange juice until smooth. Drizzle the glaze over the cooled cake.

# Chapter 3

# Pies
# and Tarts

Apple pie may be as American as baseball and prom night, but you won't find a traditional apple pie on these pages. What you'll find instead is Christine's Apple Tart (page 92), a delectable creation similar to a French apple tart but with only 261 calories and 5.9 grams of fat per serving. We think such innovation is typically American, not to mention absolutely mouth-watering.

Such is the case with all the pies in this chapter. They are lower in fat than most pies you'll run across, but taste just as—or more—delicious!

Many of our pies are made with graham cracker or granola crusts. Made the Dr. Cookie way, these are far lower in fat and calories than conventional pastry crusts. In other recipes, we rely on crisp rice cereal and chocolate cookie crumbs for crusts. We fill the crusts with luscious, juicy fruit and lightly sweetened low-fat cheese mixtures. Because we have a fondness for frozen pies (they're so easy to make ahead of time!), we also fill several crusts with frozen yogurt mixed with yummy ingredients such as candy canes and chocolate chips.

Certainly American desserts would be in a sad state without pies, but American dessert eaters don't need the fat and calories in most of them. What they need are low-fat, full-flavored pies made the Dr. Cookie way!

Think about it. *A traditional pie crust made with flour and shortening has 92 grams of fat. Divide that into eight servings of pie, discounting the filling, and you come up with nearly 12 grams of fat per slice. In comparison, a traditional graham cracker crust has 11 grams of fat per serving—not much better. But Dr. Cookie's Graham Cracker Crust has just over 6 grams of fat. And the granola variation is virtually fat-free.*

*We buy granola in bulk at the grocery store, making sure to buy nonfat granola with no nuts. The nuts instantly convert the granola into a fat-laden product.*

10 graham crackers (rectangles)
3 tablespoons margarine, melted

Preheat the oven to 350°F. Coat an 8- or 9-inch pie plate with nonstick cooking spray.

Using a rolling pin, crush the graham crackers between 2 sheets of wax paper or put them inside a sealable plastic bag. Roll the rolling pin over the bag until the crackers are crumbs. Alternatively, coarsely grind the graham crackers by pulsing them briefly in a food processor.

Combine the graham cracker crumbs with the margarine, using a fork or your fingertips to blend. Spread the mixture over the bottom and up the sides of the pie plate, pressing with your fingers to smooth it out.

Bake the crust for 8 to 10 minutes or until firm. Cool completely before serving.

1 cup nonfat granola

Coat an 8- or 9-inch pie plate with nonstick cooking spray.

Pour the granola into the prepared pie plate. As you pour in the filling, the granola will naturally cover the bottom and go up the sides of the plate.

Complete the preparation of the filled pie as directed in the recipe.

# Dr. Cookie's Graham Cracker Crust

Yield: 8 servings; makes one 8- or 9-inch pie crust

Calories per serving: 113

Fat per serving: 6.6 grams

Percent of calories from fat: 53%

# Dr. Cookie's Granola Crust

Yield: 8 servings; makes one 8- or 9-inch pie crust

Calories per serving: 38

Fat per serving: 1 gram

Percent of calories from fat: 23%

# Berry Good Cream Pie

**Yield:** 8 servings

**Calories per serving (filling only):** 92

**Fat per serving (filling only):** 1 gram

**Percent of calories from fat (filling only):** 9%

Use whatever berries are fresh and plentiful for this delightful chilled pie. We usually use the same kind of berry for the filling and topping as is in the yogurt, but there is no reason why you could not mix, say, blueberries into strawberry yogurt and top the pie with a combination of fresh blueberries and strawberries. The possibilities are endless. It's important to use gelatin-free yogurt, particularly since you are adding gelatin to the filling. Otherwise it will be unpleasantly rubbery. We use Yoplait or Dannon yogurt when looking for brands without gelatin, but use your favorite brand as long as you check the label.

- 1 tablespoon cold water
- 1 1¼-ounce package unflavored gelatin (about 2 teaspoons)
- 3 tablespoons boiling water
- 1 cup nonfat quark or low-fat cottage cheese (see Note)
- 1 cup low-fat gelatin-free raspberry, blackberry, blueberry, or strawberry yogurt
- ¼ cup sugar
- 2 cups raspberries, blackberries, blueberries, or strawberries
- 1 baked and cooled Dr. Cookie's Graham Cracker Crust or Dr. Cookie's Granola Crust (page 85)

Put the cold water in a custard cup or small bowl and sprinkle the gelatin over the surface. Allow the gelatin to soften for about 60 seconds. Pour the boiling water into the custard cup and stir until the gelatin dissolves completely. Cool slightly.

Whisk together the quark or cottage cheese, yogurt, and sugar. Add the gelatin and whisk again. Gently fold 1 cup of berries into the filling and then scrape it into the prepared pie crust.

Arrange the remaining cup of berries on top of the filling. Chill the pie for at least 4 hours before serving.

~~

**Note** Quark is a mild white cheese with blander flavor but similar texture to ricotta. Look for it in the dairy or health food section of the grocery store or buy it in a natural foods store. If you cannot find it, substitute low-fat or nonfat cottage cheese that has been processed until smooth in a blender or food processor.

We're very proud of our delicious Strawberry Whip—and as good as it is eaten plain, it makes a terrific pie filling.

  1  recipe Strawberry Whip (page 112)
  1  baked and cooled Dr. Cookie's Graham Cracker Crust (page 85)
  Fresh strawberries, for garnish

Spoon the whip into the baked pie crust. Freeze the pie for at least 4 hours or overnight. Garnish with fresh strawberries just before serving.

# Frozen Strawberry Cream Pie

<u>Yield:</u> 8 servings

<u>Calories per serving:</u> 228

<u>Fat per serving:</u> 6.6 grams

<u>Percent of calories from fat:</u> 26%

# Peach Almond Cream Pie

Yield: 8 servings

Calories per serving (filling only):
104

Fat per serving (filling only):
1.5 grams

Percent of calories from fat (filling only): 13%

We love the flavor combination of almonds and peaches. This pie is, in our humble estimation, peachy keen!

1 tablespoon cold water
1 1¼-ounce package unflavored gelatin (about 2 teaspoons)
3 tablespoons boiling water
1 cup nonfat quark or low-fat cottage cheese (see Note, page 86)
1 cup low-fat gelatin-free peach yogurt
¼ cup sugar
¼ teaspoon almond extract
1 cup peeled and diced peaches (about 1 to 2 peaches)
¼ cup slivered almonds
1 baked and cooled Dr. Cookie's Graham Cracker Crust or Dr. Cookie's Granola Crust (page 85)

Put the cold water in a custard cup or small bowl and sprinkle the gelatin over the surface. Allow the gelatin to soften for about 60 seconds. Pour the boiling water into the custard cup and stir until the gelatin dissolves completely. Cool slightly.

Whisk together the quark or cottage cheese, yogurt, and sugar. Add the gelatin and almond extract and whisk again. Gently fold the peaches and 2 tablespoons of the almonds into the filling, then scrape it into the prepared pie crust.

Sprinkle the remaining almonds on top of the filling. Chill the pie for at least 4 hours before serving.

*This light, not-too-sweet treat is made with an uncooked nonfat granola crust and nonfat yogurt. This makes it practically fat-free yet delicious enough for the most discriminating dessert lover.*

1 medium apple, unpeeled and chopped

½ teaspoon ground cinnamon

3 tablespoons orange juice concentrate

¼ cup golden raisins

1 tablespoon cold water

1 1¼-ounce package unflavored gelatin (about 2 teaspoons)

3 tablespoons boiling water

1 cup low-fat cottage cheese

2 tablespoons sugar

1 cup nonfat gelatin-free plain yogurt

1 teaspoon vanilla extract

1 cup nonfat granola

Put the chopped apple in a microwave-safe dish and sprinkle with cinnamon. Microwave on high power for about 2 minutes or until the apple is soft. Stir the orange juice concentrate and raisins with the apple and set aside.

Put the cold water in a custard cup or small bowl and sprinkle the gelatin over the surface. Allow the gelatin to soften for about 60 seconds. Pour the boiling water into the custard cup and stir until the gelatin dissolves completely. Cool slightly.

Process the cottage cheese and sugar in a food processor or blender until smooth. Add the yogurt, vanilla, and gelatin and process again just until mixed. Gently fold the apple mixture into the cottage cheese mixture.

Coat an 8- or 9-inch pie plate with nonstick cooking spray. Pour the granola into the plate. Scrape the filling into the pie plate and as you do, the granola will work up the sides of the pie plate to form a ''crust.'' Chill the pie for at least 4 hours before serving.

# Apple Yogurt Pie

<u>Yield:</u> 8 servings

<u>Calories per serving:</u> 114

<u>Fat per serving:</u> 1 gram

<u>Percent of calories from fat:</u> 7%

# Chocolate Cream Pie

**Yield:** 8 servings

**Calories per serving (filling only):**
100

**Fat per serving (filling only):**
0

**Percent of calories from fat (filling only):** 0

In the dairy section of the supermarket, we discovered a whipped topping made with skim milk. It's fun to use because it comes in a pressurized can and is easy to "squirt" on this yummy chocolate pie.

    1 tablespoon cold water
    1 1¼-ounce package unflavored gelatin (about 2 teaspoons)
    3 tablespoons boiling water
    1 cup skim milk
    1 cup nonfat gelatin-free plain yogurt
    ¼ cup sugar
    1 3.9-ounce package instant chocolate pudding mix
    1 baked and cooled Dr. Cookie's Graham Cracker Crust (page 85)
    Nonfat whipped topping

Put the cold water in a custard cup or small bowl and sprinkle the gelatin over the surface. Allow the gelatin to soften for about 60 seconds. Pour the boiling water into the custard cup and stir until the gelatin dissolves completely. Cool slightly.

Beat the milk and yogurt with an electric mixer until smooth. Add the sugar and pudding mix and beat at medium speed for about 1 minute. Add the gelatin mixture and beat well. Pour the mixture into the pie crust. Chill for 2 to 3 hours before serving. Serve with nonfat whipped topping.

This differs from a traditional pumpkin pie because we rely on low-fat ricotta cheese rather than three or four eggs for texture and flavor. Plus, plain nonfat granola forms the crust. Unsweetened pumpkin puree is an easy product to use and find—and is one of the few that is just as good if not better than fresh. Pumpkin is a terrific source of beta-carotene, which converts to vitamin A, and fiber. In fact, because this pie is so nutritious and only mildly sweet, we sometimes eat it for breakfast.

# Pumpkin Ricotta Pie

Yield: 8 servings

Calories per serving: 219

Fat per serving: 2.3 grams

Percent of calories from fat: 9%

1 cup nonfat granola

1 large egg

2 large egg whites

¾ cup packed brown sugar

1½ teaspoons pumpkin pie spice

¼ teaspoon salt

⅔ cup evaporated skim milk

1 cup low-fat ricotta cheese

2 cups unsweetened pumpkin puree (one 16-ounce can)

1 teaspoon vanilla extract

½ cup golden raisins

Preheat the oven to 375°F. Coat an 8- or 9-inch pie plate with nonstick cooking spray and sprinkle granola over the bottom of the pie plate.

Beat the egg, egg whites, and brown sugar with an electric mixer until smooth and fluffy. Add the pie spice, salt, skim milk, ricotta, pumpkin puree, and vanilla and beat well. Fold the raisins into the filling.

Scrape the filling into the pie plate and as you do, the granola will work up the sides of the pie plate to form a "crust." Bake the pie for about 45 minutes or until the filling looks set and a knife inserted near the center comes out clean. Cool completely on a wire rack before serving, or chill the pie until ready to serve.

# Christine's Apple Tart

**Yield:** 8 servings

**Calories per serving:** 261

**Fat per serving:** 5.9 grams

**Percent of calories from fat:** 20%

Chris is fit and slender—and an incredible cook. We thank her for sharing this fantastic tart with us, which is a breeze to make if you have a food processor. Because the tart is so pretty, we highly recommend carrying it to the table and showing it off before slicing it.

- 4 tablespoons (½ stick) margarine, cut into ½-inch pieces
- 1 cup unbleached all-purpose flour
- ¼ cup packed brown sugar
- 1 large egg white
- ½ cup old-fashioned rolled oats
- 5 large, tart apples, such as Granny Smiths
- 2 tablespoons sugar
- 2 tablespoons Grand Marnier
- 1 teaspoon ground cinnamon
- ½ teaspoon grated nutmeg
- 1½ teaspoons lemon juice
- ½ cup orange marmalade, sweetened only with fruit juice

Preheat the oven to 350°F. and coat a 9-inch tart pan or springform pan with nonstick cooking spray.

Put the margarine, flour, and brown sugar in the bowl of a food processor fitted with a metal blade and process just to a uniform consistency. Add the egg white and process briefly. Add the oats to the dough and mix them in with a fork.

Press the dough into the bottom and up the sides of the tart pan. Bake the crust for 10 minutes. Remove from the oven and set aside to cool.

Peel, core, and quarter 3 apples. Process them in the food processor until finely chopped but not pureed. Put the apples in a saucepan with 1 tablespoon sugar and 1 tablespoon Grand Marnier. Cook over medium heat, stirring constantly, for 20 to 25 minutes or until all the liquid is absorbed and the apples are soft.

Peel the remaining 2 apples and slice them very thin. Toss the apple slices with the remaining tablespoon of sugar, cinnamon, nutmeg, and lemon juice. Mix the marmalade with the remaining tablespoon of Grand Marnier in a separate bowl.

Spread the cooked apples on the prebaked crust. Arrange the sliced apples over the filling. Brush the marmalade over the sliced apples.

Bake the tart for 30 to 40 minutes or until the crust is browned. Cool for 10 minutes before serving, or serve at room temperature.

# Frozen Chocolate Chip Mint Pie

Yield: 12 servings

Calories per serving: 220

Fat per serving: 5.3 grams

Percent of calories from fat: 22%

*While the stores seem to stock more and more nonfat and low-fat frozen desserts, we have yet to see a chocolate chip mint pie. Dr Cookie's prescription for this deficiency is this cool and minty pie—but leave out the food coloring if you prefer.*

1½ tablespoons margarine

½ cup semisweet chocolate chips

1 teaspoon vanilla extract

1½ cups crisp rice cereal

½ gallon nonfat frozen vanilla yogurt, softened

½ teaspoon peppermint extract

Green food coloring (optional)

½ cup mini semisweet chocolate chips

Wrap the removable bottom of a 9-inch springform pan with plastic wrap and then assemble the pan.

Melt the margarine in a small saucepan over medium heat. Add the chocolate chips, take the pan from the heat, and stir until melted. Add the vanilla and stir again. Add the cereal and stir gently to coat the cereal.

Scrape the cereal into the springform pan and spread it over the bottom.

Combine the softened frozen yogurt, peppermint extract, a few drops of food coloring, if desired, and the mini chocolate chips. Spoon the yogurt over the crust and smooth it in the pan with the back of a spoon or a spatula. Freeze the pie for at least 4 hours.

Remove the pie from the freezer about 5 minutes before serving. To serve, run a knife around the outside edge of the pan, release the springform pan and lift the pie off the bottom of the springform pan with a metal spatula. Peel off the plastic and serve the pie on a pretty plate.

# Frozen Peppermint Pie

**Yield:** 12 servings

**Calories per serving:** 220

**Fat per serving:** 3.3 grams

**Percent of calories from fat:** 14%

*G*ive *yourself an extra-special present at Christmastime: a low-fat frozen peppermint pie that tastes as rich and sweet as a holiday dessert should. We have trouble finding these mini candy canes in the stores except during the December holidays, but if you crave the pie at other times of year, simply chop up peppermint hard candies to equal about a half-cup.*

1 ½ tablespoons margarine

½ cup semisweet chocolate chips

1 teaspoon vanilla extract

1 ½ cups crisp rice cereal

18 2-inch candy canes

½ gallon nonfat frozen vanilla yogurt, softened

½ teaspoon peppermint extract

Red food coloring (optional)

Wrap the removable bottom of a 9-inch springform pan with plastic wrap and then assemble the pan.

Melt the margarine in a small saucepan over medium heat. Add the chocolate chips, take the pan from the heat, and stir until melted. Add the vanilla and stir again. Add the cereal and stir gently to coat the cereal.

Scrape the cereal into the springform pan and spread it over the bottom.

Coarsely chop 6 candy canes. Reserve the rest for garnish. Combine the softened frozen yogurt, peppermint extract, a few drops of food coloring, if desired, and the chopped candy canes. Spoon the yogurt over the crust and smooth it in the pan with the back of a spoon or a spatula. Freeze the pie for at least 4 hours.

Remove the pie from the freezer about 5 minutes before serving. To serve, run a knife around the outside edge of the pan, release the springform pan, and lift the pie off the bottom of the springform pan with a metal spatula. Peel off the plastic and serve the pie on a pretty plate garnished with the remaining candy canes.

**W**e make a simple crust with cream-filled chocolate sandwich cookies that, combined with the chocolaty filling, make this dessert taste like old-fashioned fudge pops. We use Hydrox cookies because they do not contain animal fats, which we always try to avoid.

6   chocolate sandwich cookies, such as Hydrox

1   tablespoon cold water

1   1¼-ounce package unflavored gelatin (about 2 teaspoons)

3   tablespoons boiling water

1¼  cups skim milk

1   cup low-fat gelatin-free coffee or vanilla yogurt

¼   cup sugar

1   3.9-ounce package instant chocolate pudding mix

Coat an 8-inch springform pan with nonstick cooking spray.

Put the cookies in the bowl of a food processor fitted with a metal blade and process to crumbs. Press the crumbs into the bottom of the springform pan.

Put the cold water in a custard cup or small bowl and sprinkle the gelatin over the surface. Allow the gelatin to soften for about 60 seconds. Pour the boiling water into the custard cup and stir until the gelatin dissolves completely. Cool slightly.

Beat the milk and yogurt with an electric mixer set at high until smooth. Add the sugar and pudding mix and beat at medium speed for about 1 minute. Add the gelatin mixture and beat well. Pour the mixture over the cookie crust. Freeze the pie for at least 4 hours.

Remove the pie from the freezer about 5 minutes before serving. To serve, run a knife around the outside edge of the pan, release the springform pan, and lift the pie off the bottom of the springform pan with a metal spatula. Serve it on a pretty plate.

For an interesting variation, top each slice with one meringue cookie (page 38).

# Frozen Fudge Pop Pie

Yield: 8 servings

Calories per serving: 175

Fat per serving: 2.3 grams

Percent of calories from fat: 12%

# Dr. Cookie's Cookies 'n Cream Frozen Pie

**Yield:** 12 servings

**Calories per serving:**
185 made with Dr. Cookie's Chocolate Chip Cookies (page 23); 236 made with Dr. Cookie's Chocolate Chip–Oatmeal Cookies (available through mail order)

**Fat per serving:**
2 grams made with Dr. Cookie's Chocolate Chip Cookies; 5 grams made with Dr. Cookie's Chocolate Chip–Oatmeal Cookies

**Percent of calories from fat:**
10% made with Dr. Cookie's Chocolate Chip Cookies; 19% made with Dr. Cookie's Chocolate Chip–Oatmeal Cookies

If you love chocolate chip cookies as much as we do, you will love this simple pie. Use Dr. Cookie's Chocolate Chip Cookies or your favorite high-quality cookies. Check the package label to make sure they do not contain animal fats and are not too high in fat and calories. To mail order Dr. Cookie's Chocolate Chip–Oatmeal cookies, see page 217. They have 139 calories and 6 grams of fat each, but we think they are worth the extra fat and calories every now and then.

      10  3-inch Dr. Cookie's Chocolate Chip Cookies (page 23) or other chocolate chip cookies
      ½  gallon nonfat frozen vanilla yogurt, softened

Wrap the removable bottom of a 9-inch springform pan with plastic wrap and then assemble the pan.

Put 7 cookies in the bowl of a food processor fitted with a metal blade and process to crumbs. Press the crumbs into the bottom of the springform pan.

Put the remaining 3 cookies in the food processor and process until coarsely chopped. Stir the chopped cookies into the softened yogurt. Spoon the yogurt over the crust and smooth it in the pan with the back of a spoon or a spatula. Freeze the pie for at least 4 hours.

Remove the pie from the freezer about 5 minutes before serving. To serve, run a knife around the outside edge of the pan, release the springform pan, and lift the pie off the bottom of the springform pan with a metal spatula. Peel off the plastic and serve the pie on a pretty plate.

# Chapter 4

# Fruit Desserts

**H**ave you ever tasted a peach during the height of summer? Plucked a strawberry from beneath the dewy leaves of a strawberry plant on a warm June morning? Or bitten into a crisp, juicy apple from a country orchard in October? These are the sort of eating experiences that make us fruit fanatics. The vitamins, minerals, complex carbohydrates, and dietary fiber available in fresh fruit make us fruit disciples.

We cannot imagine a better dessert than a piece of perfect fruit. To us, perfection means fruit that is organically grown and lovingly tended until it reaches its optimal ripeness. But we also love to cook and create, and so have devised a number of recipes that fall into the general category of fruit desserts. None is hard to make; all are low in fat and calories. We urge you to use fruit when it is in season where you live. Don't force the seasons by buying high-priced imported blueberries in February for the Dazzle Berry Cobbler (page 104) when you can just as easily make luscious Hot Apple Gingerbread (page 103) or comforting Rice Pudding with Raisins (page 106). Wait until July for the blueberries.

It's important to eat lots of fruit. We find it interesting that in a recent issue of *American Family Physician* magazine, the top four baby foods were fruit: bananas, applesauce, pears, and peaches. The fifth was sweet potatoes. Babies don't mind eating fruit for supper. In fact, the amount of fruit they consume can be a lesson for us older folks. Babies get a good ration of vitamin C, beta-carotene, complex carbohydrates, and fiber from all that fruit. Shouldn't you?

**A** compote is a fruit dessert cooked in syrup, but who will notice if we stray from the definition and omit the syrup? This simple, one-serving fruit dessert is filling and satisfying, and especially great with a scoop of vanilla nonfat frozen yogurt or low-fat ice milk. Multiply the ingredients many times over depending on who's hungry. It is good freshly made, leftover, reheated, or cold.

1 medium apple, unpeeled and cut into ½-inch pieces

2 tablespoons raisins

About ½ teaspoon ground cinnamon

Put about ½ inch of water in a heavy saucepan and add the apple and raisins. Mix well and sprinkle with cinnamon, adding a little more than ½ teaspoon, if desired. Stir gently.

Cover the pan and cook the fruit over low heat for about 20 minutes or until the apple softens. Remove the pan from the heat and let it sit, covered, for 15 to 20 minutes before serving.

# Hot Apple-Raisin Compote

Yield: 1 serving

Calories per serving: about 160

Fat per serving: 0

Percent of calories from fat: 0

# Peaches 'n Cream

Yield: 1 serving

Calories per serving:
105, not including crushed cookies

Fat per serving: 0

Percent of calories from fat: 0

**W**hat is more sensuous than a ripe, fragrant peach? And we mean those peaches available only in August, ripened on the tree by the sun and best eaten soon after picking. No hothouse varieties for us! We like to indulge in these luscious fruits outside in the summer sun, letting the sweet juice drip down our chins. Taking summer peaches inside for fancier treatment is easy and delicious, too. Here is a variation on fresh peaches and sweet cream that relies on low-fat sour cream or yogurt.

2  tablespoons packed brown sugar
1  tablespoon Amaretto or 2 teaspoons almond extract
1  cup low-fat sour cream or plain yogurt
4  large ripe peaches, peeled and sliced
Crushed Amaretti cookies or slivered almonds, for topping

Stir together the brown sugar, Amaretto, and sour cream. Spoon over sliced peaches in individual bowls and top with crushed cookies or almonds.

$H$ere's another way to enjoy one of summer's best crops. Substitute your favorite fruit-flavored frozen yogurt for the raspberry—which happens to be our favorite.

- 1  scoop raspberry nonfat frozen yogurt
- 1  large peach, peeled and sliced

Put the yogurt in an individual serving dish and top with peach slices.

# Frozen Melba

Yield: 1 serving

Calories per serving: 135

Fat per serving: 0

Percent of calories from fat: 0

$T$he original peach melba was made, no doubt, with ice cream. Ours tastes just as good and has only half the fat.

- 2  scoops vanilla ice milk or vanilla nonfat frozen yogurt
- 2  to 3 large ripe peaches, peeled and sliced
- ¼  cup Raspberry Sauce (page 76)

Put 1 scoop of ice milk or yogurt into each of 2 individual serving dishes. Arrange peach slices around each scoop and top each with about 2 tablespoons of sauce.

# Peach Melba

Yield: 2 servings

Calories per serving: 180

Fat per serving: 0

Percent of calories from fat: 0

# Cran-Apple Crisp

**Yield:** 9 servings

**Calories per serving:** 233

**Fat per serving:** 6 grams

**Percent of calories from fat:** 23%

*W*e love how Granny Smith apples stay firm and tart in this recipe, but you can use any firm, tart apple. Choose the ones in season where you live for ultimate freshness.

1½ cups old-fashioned rolled oats

¼ cup packed brown sugar

¼ cup (½ stick) margarine, melted

¼ cup unbleached all-purpose flour

¼ teaspoon salt

¾ cup granulated sugar

1 teaspoon ground cinnamon

1 tablespoon cornstarch

3 cups chopped unpeeled tart apples (3 to 4 large apples)

2 cups fresh or frozen and thawed cranberries

Preheat the oven to 350°F. Coat an 8-inch square pan with nonstick cooking spray.

Combine the oats, brown sugar, margarine, flour, and salt in a small bowl. Stir well and set aside.

Whisk together the granulated sugar, cinnamon, and cornstarch. Add the apples and cranberries and toss well. Put the mixture in the pan and sprinkle the oat topping evenly over it. Bake for 35 to 45 minutes or until the fruit is hot and bubbly and the oats are nicely browned.

As good as this gingery dessert is warm from the oven, it reaches incredible heights when topped with vanilla nonfat frozen yogurt.

4 cups sliced unpeeled firm apples (about 4 apples)
¼ cup packed brown sugar
¾ cup unsweetened apple juice
2 teaspoons cornstarch
1 tablespoon cold water
1 large egg
¼ cup granulated sugar
¼ cup molasses
2 tablespoons vegetable oil
½ cup buttermilk
1 cup unbleached all-purpose flour
½ teaspoon baking soda
½ teaspoon baking powder
¾ teaspoon ground ginger
¼ teaspoon grated nutmeg
¼ teaspoon salt

Preheat the oven to 350°F. and coat an 8-inch square pan with nonstick cooking spray.

Combine the apples, brown sugar, and apple juice in a saucepan and cook over low heat for about 10 minutes or until the apples begin to soften.

Stir the cornstarch and water together until smooth. Add to the apples and cook for a few minutes longer until slightly thickened. Pour the apples into the prepared 8-inch pan.

Beat the egg, granulated sugar, molasses, oil, and buttermilk with an electric mixer set at high until smooth. Add the flour, baking soda, baking powder, spices, and salt and beat until well mixed. Pour the gingerbread batter over the apples.

Bake for about 30 minutes or until the gingerbread is nicely browned.

# Hot Apple Gingerbread

<u>Yield:</u> 9 servings

<u>Calories per serving:</u> 188

<u>Fat per serving:</u> 4 grams

<u>Percent of calories from fat:</u> 19%

# Dazzle Berry Cobbler

**Yield:** 9 servings

**Calories per serving:** 200

**Fat per serving:** 4 grams

**Percent of calories from fat:** 18%

We use more blueberries than cranberries or blackberries in this dessert, but you can rearrange the amounts to suit your own tastes or available fruit. You might like to substitute another berry, such as raspberries, for one of the choices here. Fresh berries are a plentiful crop where we live in the Pacific Northwest, but the dessert is equally tasty made with frozen unsweetened berries instead. Let them thaw before cooking. The cobbler is topped with spoonfuls of dumplinglike batter and baked until bubbling. This is sure to "dazzle" your family and friends.

¾ cup plus 1 tablespoon sugar

1 tablespoon cornstarch

1½ teaspoons ground cinnamon

½ teaspoon grated nutmeg

2 cups fresh or frozen and thawed blueberries

1 cup fresh or frozen and thawed cranberries

1 cup fresh or frozen and thawed blackberries

1 tablespoon orange juice

1 cup peeled and chopped apple (about 1 apple)

1 large egg

2 tablespoons vegetable oil

½ cup buttermilk

1 cup unbleached all-purpose flour

1½ teaspoons baking powder

¼ teaspoon salt

Preheat the oven to 350°F. and coat an 8-inch square pan with nonstick cooking spray.

Combine ¾ cup sugar and the cornstarch in a medium saucepan and add 1 teaspoon cinnamon, the nutmeg, berries, and orange juice. Bring to a boil over medium-high heat, stirring constantly, for 1 to 2 minutes or until the mixture thickens. Stir the chopped apple into the mixture and pour it into the prepared 8-inch pan.

Beat the egg, oil, remaining 1 tablespoon sugar, and buttermilk with an electric mixer set at high until smooth. Add the flour, baking powder, remaining ½ teaspoon cinnamon, and salt and beat just until combined.

Spoon the batter in 8 or 9 spoonfuls over the top of the fruit mixture. Bake for about 30 minutes or until the batter is golden brown and the fruit is hot and bubbly. Cool for 10 minutes before serving.

*Small Italian prune plums—also called fresh prunes or Italian prunes—are a freestone variety of plum, which means the flesh separates readily from the pit, with purple skin and firm yellow flesh. They are easy to work with and hold up well when baked. This makes them a perfect choice for this lovely fruit crisp that is as yummy served at room temperature as it is served warm from the oven. Other European-style plums do well, too. Juicier Japanese plums, which have red or yellow skin, are not as successful for baking, but make great eating out of hand.*

1 ½ cups old-fashioned rolled oats

¼ cup packed brown sugar

4 tablespoons (½ stick) margarine, melted

½ cup unbleached all-purpose flour

¼ teaspoon salt

5 cups diced plums (about 20 to 25 plums)

¾ cup granulated sugar

1 teaspoon ground cinnamon

½ teaspoon grated nutmeg

Preheat the oven to 350°F. and coat an 8-inch square pan with nonstick cooking spray.

Combine the oats, brown sugar, margarine, ¼ cup flour, and salt in a small bowl. Stir well and set aside.

Toss the plums with the granulated sugar, remaining ¼ cup flour, cinnamon, and nutmeg. Put the plum mixture in the prepared pan and sprinkle the oat topping evenly over it.

Bake for about 45 minutes or until the fruit is hot and bubbly and the oats are nicely browned.

# Plum Crisp

**Yield:** 9 servings

**Calories per serving:** 252

**Fat per serving:** 6 grams

**Percent of calories from fat:** 21%

# Rice Pudding with Raisins

Yield: 8 servings

Calories per serving: 135

Fat per serving: 1.3 grams

Percent of calories from fat: 9%

Rice pudding is classic comfort food—and our healthful version is as warm and reassuring as a cozy quilt. Brown sugar and plump raisins sweeten it, and brown rice provides body and plenty of good-for-you fiber. Try it warm with a spoonful of nonfat yogurt. Or save some for tomorrow. It's great leftover, warmed up or eaten cold.

2 large eggs, at room temperature

½ cup packed brown sugar

2 cups skim milk, at room temperature

1 teaspoon vanilla extract

½ teaspoon ground cinnamon

¼ teaspoon grated nutmeg

⅔ cup raisins

2 cups hot cooked brown rice

Preheat the oven to 325°F. Coat an 8-inch square pan with nonstick cooking spray.

Beat the eggs and brown sugar with an electric mixer set on medium until smooth. Add the milk, vanilla, cinnamon, and nutmeg and beat again. Stir the raisins and hot rice into the mixture until blended.

Scrape the pudding into the pan and bake for 50 to 60 minutes. Stir the pudding after 15 minutes and again after 30 minutes. Spoon off any water that accumulates on the top of the pudding. The pudding is done when it looks set and a knife inserted in the center comes out clean. Cool the pudding in the pan for 10 minutes before serving. Store any leftover pudding in the refrigerator.

We say "thank goodness!"—here's a light Thanksgiving dessert. Make this with your favorite cranberry-orange relish and refrigerate or freeze it before serving. Chilled creams have a softer texture than frozen ones and both are light, refreshing, and most welcome after the annual mega feast—or anytime of year.

½ cup orange juice

1 tablespoon cold water

1 1¼-ounce package unflavored gelatin (about 2 teaspoons)

3 tablespoons boiling water

⅔ cup nonfat dry milk

¼ cup sugar

¾ cup nonfat gelatin-free raspberry yogurt

½ cup cranberry-orange relish

4 teaspoons cranberry relish (optional), for garnish

4 thinly sliced orange rounds (optional), for garnish

Pour the orange juice in the bowl of an electric mixer and put the bowl and the beaters in the freezer for about 30 minutes or until ice begins to form around the edges of the bowl.

About 5 minutes before removing the bowl from the freezer, put the cold water in a custard cup or small bowl and sprinkle the gelatin over the surface. Allow the gelatin to soften for about 60 seconds. Pour the boiling water into the custard cup and stir until the gelatin dissolves completely. Cool slightly.

Take the bowl and beaters from the freezer and add the dry milk. Beat on low speed for about 60 seconds. Increase the speed to high and beat until stiff peaks form. Add the sugar and beat for 60 seconds longer. Finally, add the softened gelatin and yogurt and beat just until combined. Fold in the cranberry-orange relish.

Spoon the cream into 4 stemmed glasses and chill or freeze for several hours. Garnish each dessert with a teaspoonful of cranberry relish and a twist of orange.

# Cranberry-Orange Cream

Yield: 4 servings

Calories per serving: 200

Fat per serving: .5 gram

Percent of calories from fat: 2%

# Pared-Down Pavlova

Yield: 2 servings

Calories per serving: 165

Fat per serving: 1 gram

Percent of calories from fat: 5%

Traditional pavlova is a rich dessert combining meringue, whipped cream, and fruit. We pared it down by using low-fat yogurt rather than whipped cream and our own fat-free meringue cookies. Fresh raspberries are great, but you could also use Raspberry Sauce (page 76). Kiwis are startlingly pretty and taste of strawberries and sunshine. Their fuzzy outer skin is edible and does not have to be peeled, but you may do so if you prefer. The dessert can be multiplied many times over, depending on the number of cookies, amount of raspberries, and number of dessert lovers present.

1 cup fresh raspberries
¾ cup low-fat gelatin-free raspberry yogurt
2 meringue cookies (page 38)
1 kiwi, sliced

Divide the raspberries evenly between 2 serving bowls. Top the raspberries with yogurt. Set a cookie on top of each scoop of yogurt and arrange the kiwi slices around the yogurt.

There are lots of good reasons why you should serve this dessert after a robust meal. First, it's deliciously light; second, it can be made well ahead of time; and third, pineapple is a good source of vitamin C and the trace mineral manganese, which helps to strengthen our bones. Be sure to use canned pineapple for the recipe. Fresh pineapple and gelatin do not bond and you will be left with a soupy mess.

- 1   15-ounce can unsweetened crushed pineapple, undrained
- 1   1¼-ounce package unflavored gelatin (about 2 teaspoons)
- 1¾ cups low-fat gelatin-free piña colada yogurt
- ½  teaspoon coconut extract
- ½  teaspoon rum or rum extract
- ¼  cup unsweetened shredded coconut

Drain the pineapple and reserve the juice. Measure the juice and add enough water to equal ¾ cup liquid. Stir and then pour ¼ cup of the pineapple juice into a small bowl and sprinkle the gelatin over the surface. Allow the gelatin to soften for about 60 seconds.

Bring the remaining ½ cup of juice to a boil and pour into the bowl, then stir until the gelatin dissolves completely. Cool slightly and refrigerate the mixture until it is the consistency of egg whites.

Pour the cold liquid into the bowl of an electric mixer and beat on high speed until fluffy. Add the crushed pineapple, yogurt, coconut extract, rum, and shredded coconut and stir until blended.

Spoon the mixture into 4 stemmed glasses and chill for at least 2 to 3 hours before serving. Garnish with tropical imagination.

# Pineapple Coconut Parfait

Yield: 4 servings

Calories per serving: 187

Fat per serving: 2.7 grams

Percent of calories from fat: 13%

# Lava Flow

Yield: 4 servings

Calories per serving: 219

Fat per serving: 2.7 grams

Percent of calories from fat: 11%

We first tasted a Lava Flow in a wonderful restaurant on the magical island of Maui in Hawaii. There, it's a drink combining piña coladas and strawberry daiquiris. Our version is less potent but just as delicious. Easy-as-a-wink strawberry sauce is poured into tunnels carved from the sides of the Pineapple Coconut Parfait described on page 109. The colorful sauce evokes red-hot lava flowing down the sides of a volcano. The sauce alone, which yields just over a cup, is great with other desserts, too. We make it all the time with or without the lime rind.

16 ounces frozen unsweetened strawberries, thawed but not drained, or 1 pint fresh strawberries mixed with 3 tablespoons water or lime, lemon, or orange juice

2 tablespoons confectioners' sugar

½ teaspoon grated lime rind (optional)

1 recipe Pineapple Coconut Parfait (page 109)

Combine the strawberries, juice, sugar, and lime rind in a blender or food processor. Blend until smooth. Refrigerate the sauce until ready to use.

Prepare the parfaits according to the recipe instructions. Refrigerate until ready to use.

Just before serving, slide a kitchen knife between a parfait and the side of the glass to make a tunnel almost as long as the glass is deep. Make 4 tunnels around the parfait. Repeat with the remaining 3 parfaits. Spoon about a tablespoon of sauce into each tunnel so that it fills the tunnel. Serve right away. Store any leftover sauce in the refrigerator for another use.

**A**s the raisins soak in the rum, they plump up and absorb the liquid. We mix these seductive fruits with yogurt and a little sugar for a wonderful dessert.

 ½ cup raisins

 2 tablespoons dark rum

 ½ cup plus 1 tablespoon cold water

 1 1¼-ounce package unflavored gelatin (about 2 teaspoons)

 3 tablespoons boiling water

 ⅔ cup nonfat dry milk

 ¼ cup sugar

 1 cup low-fat gelatin-free vanilla yogurt

Combine the raisins and rum in a small bowl and let sit for at least 3 hours.

Pour ½ cup cold water in the bowl of an electric mixer and put the bowl and the beaters in the freezer for about 30 minutes or until ice begins to form around the edges of the bowl.

About 5 minutes before removing the bowl from the freezer, put the remaining tablespoon of cold water in a custard cup or small bowl and sprinkle the gelatin over the surface. Allow the gelatin to soften for about 60 seconds. Pour the boiling water into the custard cup and stir until the gelatin dissolves completely. Cool slightly.

Take the bowl and beaters from the freezer and add the dry milk. Beat on low speed for about 60 seconds. Increase the speed to high and beat until stiff peaks form. Add the sugar and beat for 60 seconds longer. Finally, add the softened gelatin and yogurt and beat just until combined. Fold in the rum-soaked raisins and any rum not absorbed by the raisins.

Spoon the mixture into 4 stemmed glasses and serve right away or refrigerate until serving.

# Rum Raisin Parfaits

<u>Yield:</u> 4 servings

<u>Calories per serving:</u> 140

<u>Fat per serving:</u> 1.2 grams

<u>Percent of calories from fat:</u> 8%

111

# Strawberry Whip

**Yield:** 8 servings

**Calories per serving:** 115

**Fat per serving:** 0

**Percent of calories from fat:** 0

**K**ids love this colorful whip, and come to think of it, so do we! Strawberries work well, but you could substitute other berries, too. As good as this is plain, it makes a terrific topping for your favorite summertime strawberry shortcake, in place of fat-laden whipped cream.

16 ounces frozen unsweetened strawberries, thawed but not drained

1 tablespoon cold water

1 1¼-ounce package unflavored gelatin (about 2 teaspoons)

3 tablespoons boiling water

1⅓ cups nonfat dry milk

¼ cup sugar

Drain the strawberries and reserve the juice. Measure the juice and add enough water to it to equal 1 cup. Pour the liquid into the bowl of an electric mixer and put the bowl and the beaters in the freezer for about 30 minutes or until ice begins to form around the edges of the bowl.

About 5 minutes before removing the bowl from the freezer, put the cold water in a custard cup or small bowl and sprinkle the gelatin over the surface. Allow the gelatin to soften for about 60 seconds. Pour the boiling water into the custard cup and stir until the gelatin dissolves completely. Cool slightly.

Take the bowl and beaters from the freezer and add the dry milk. Beat on low speed for about 60 seconds. Increase the speed to high and beat until stiff peaks form. Add the sugar gradually and beat for 60 seconds longer. Finally, add the softened gelatin and strawberries and beat on low speed just until combined. Serve immediately or freeze the whip and serve it as you would ice cream.

We think this trifle tastes better than the traditional English trifles we have had over the years. It's just as creamy and rich but tastes lighter and fresher. Experiment with other fruits and berries to utilize what is fresh and what you especially like. Soft fruits such as peaches and plums work best, as do all berries. To save an additional 30 calories per serving, use instant pudding mixes sweetened with aspartame or another sugar substitute.

# Trifle

Yield: 12 servings

Calories per serving: 208

Fat per serving: 0

Percent of calories from fat: 0

2  3.9-ounce packages lemon or vanilla instant pudding mix

3½ cups skim milk

2  quarts fresh or frozen strawberries

¼ to ½ cup orange juice or Grand Marnier

1  12-ounce fat-free pound cake, cut into ½-inch slices

Prepare the lemon or vanilla pudding with the skim milk as directed on the packages. Set aside.

Combine the berries with the orange juice. If using frozen berries, include some of the juice from them. The amount of juice depends on how moist you like trifle.

Arrange half the cake slices on the bottom of a 2-quart casserole, glass soufflé dish, or any attractive bowl. Glass bowls are especially pretty for trifle.

Sprinkle half the berries over the cake. Pour half the orange juice over the berries. Spoon half of the prepared pudding over the berries.

Top with the remaining pound cake, the rest of the berries, the orange juice, and the remaining pudding.

Cover the bowl and chill the trifle for at least 4 hours or overnight.

Peanut Butter–Banana Cookies (page 32)
and Chocolate Banana Brownies (page 51)

Apple Cookies (page 17)

Hippie Cookies (page 28)

Harvest Cookies (page 27)

Lemon Drops (page 29)

Tropical Treats (page 36)

Cherry-Almond Biscotti (page 42)

Dr. Cookie's Chocolate Chip Cookies (page 23)
and Heavenly Chocolate Oatmeal Cookies (page 24)

Surprise Cake (page 74)

Chocolate Decadence with Raspberry Sauce (page 76)

Apple-Cranberry Cake (page 64)

Berry Good Cream Pie (page 86)
and Christine's Apple Tart (page 92)

Lava Flow (page 110)

Carrot-Bran Muffins (page 120)
and Blueberry Muffins (page 124)

Roasted Red Pepper Bread (page 188)

Corn-Rye-Millet Bread (page 183)

Hiking Bread (page 166)

# Chapter 5

# Muffins and Biscuits

**M**uffins are the greatest. They can be made with an almost endless list of ingredients that can be mixed in almost any combination that suits your fancy. They satisfy cravings for baked goods, but by their very nature are, for the most part, low in fat and calories. Our favorites are high in fiber, too, and so tend to be on the heavy side, which we think makes them more satisfying. We also have plenty of recipes for lighter muffins.

Both muffins and biscuits, easy to prepare on short notice, turn an ordinary meal into a special one. Bring a basket of piping hot biscuits to a table laid with vegetable soup and salad, and listen for the ''oohs'' and ''ahhs.'' Ditto for freshly baked muffins, especially at the breakfast table.

The secret to making both is never to overmix the batter. Begin with room-temperature ingredients. First mix the dry ingredients in a small bowl and then the wet ingredients in a large bowl. Add the dry to the wet and stir only until combined. Lumps are okay.

Heavy muffin tins give better results than less expensive, insubstantial ones. Muffins cook for a relatively short time, and our experience has been that they bake more evenly in heavy tins.

Finally, we have discovered a foolproof method for cutting the shortening into the flour for the biscuit recipes—a cooking instruction that always baffled us. First, process the dry ingredients in a food processor for a quick two seconds and then drop the cold margarine or butter into the workbowl. Process for eight seconds longer. Perfect every time!

As you may have diagnosed, we like the flavor combination of oats and apples a lot. We also like the health benefits of the fiber supplied by both ingredients. And we love how absolutely delicious these muffins taste.

1 cup unbleached all-purpose flour

1 cup oat bran

2 teaspoons baking powder

½ teaspoon baking soda

1 teaspoon ground cinnamon

½ teaspoon grated nutmeg

1 large egg

½ cup packed brown sugar

2 tablespoons vegetable oil

1 cup natural unsweetened applesauce

¾ cup old-fashioned rolled oats

½ cup chopped unpeeled apple (1 small apple)

Preheat the oven to 400°F. Coat one 12- or two 6-muffin tins with nonstick cooking spray.

Whisk the flour with the oat bran, baking powder, baking soda, cinnamon, and nutmeg and set aside.

Beat the egg, brown sugar, and oil with an electric mixer set on medium until smooth. Add the applesauce and oats and beat again. Mix the flour and chopped apple into the batter by hand just until combined.

Spoon the batter into the muffin cups so that each is about two-thirds full. Bake for 15 to 20 minutes or until the muffins are lightly browned, puff up, and a toothpick inserted in the center comes out clean. Cool in the tin set on a wire rack for about 10 minutes. Remove the muffins from the tin and eat them warm, or let them cool completely on a wire rack.

# Applesauce Oat Bran Muffins

Yield: 12 muffins

Calories per muffin: 142

Fat per muffin: 3.6 grams

Percent of calories from fat: 23%

# Banana-Bran Muffins

Yield: 12 muffins

Calories per muffin: 97

Fat per muffin: 2 grams

Percent of calories from fat: 19%

**W**heat bran is one of the most effective insoluble fibers, which means it helps keep your body running like clockwork. As a result, bran muffins are extremely popular as breakfast food and as snacks. Unfortunately, many bran muffins are almost as high in fat as they are in fiber. Because we moisten these with banana rather than fat, we reduce the number of calories and the total fat to only 2 grams per muffin.

- ½ cup unbleached all-purpose flour
- ½ cup whole wheat flour
- 1 cup wheat bran
- 1 teaspoon baking powder
- 1 teaspoon baking soda
- 1 large egg
- ⅓ cup molasses
- 1 tablespoon vegetable oil
- ¾ cup buttermilk
- ½ cup mashed ripe banana (about 1 banana)

Preheat the oven to 400°F. Coat one 12- or two 6-muffin tins with nonstick cooking spray.

Whisk the flours with the wheat bran, baking powder, and baking soda and set aside.

Beat the egg, molasses, and oil with an electric mixer set on medium until smooth. Add the buttermilk and banana and beat again. Mix the flour into the batter by hand just until combined.

Spoon the batter into the muffin cups so that each is about two-thirds full. Bake for 15 to 20 minutes or until the muffins are lightly browned, puff up, and a toothpick inserted in the center comes out clean. Cool in the tin set on a wire rack for about 10 minutes. Remove the muffins from the tin and eat them warm, or let them cool completely on a wire rack.

We call these Sunday morning muffins because you need to set aside an extra hour for preparation. In our book, that means they are not well suited for the midweek scramble. Like the Banana-Bran Muffins on page 118, they are moistened with banana more than fat and so are relatively low in calories and fat. They also are lovely and light.

1 cup wheat bran
1 cup boiling water
1 cup unbleached all-purpose flour
1½ teaspoons baking powder
1½ teaspoons baking soda
⅓ cup nonfat dry milk
1 large egg
½ cup packed brown sugar
2 tablespoons vegetable oil
½ cup mashed ripe banana (about 1 banana)
1 teaspoon vanilla extract

Stir the wheat bran into the boiling water and let it sit for 1 hour.

Preheat the oven to 400°F. Coat one 12- or two 6-muffin tins with nonstick cooking spray.

Whisk the flour with the baking powder, baking soda, and dry milk powder and set aside.

Beat the egg, brown sugar, and oil with an electric mixer set on medium until smooth. Add the banana and vanilla and beat again. Mix the flour into the batter by hand just until combined.

Spoon the batter into the muffin cups so that each is about two-thirds full. Bake for 15 to 20 minutes or until the muffins are lightly browned, puff up, and a toothpick inserted in the center comes out clean. Cool in the tin set on a wire rack for about 10 minutes. Remove the muffins from the tin and eat them warm, or let them cool completely on a wire rack.

# Sunday Morning Banana-Bran Muffins

Yield: 12 muffins

Calories per muffin: 107

Fat per muffin: 3.1 grams

Percent of calories from fat: 26%

# Carrot-Bran Muffins

**Yield:** 12 muffins

**Calories per muffin:** 125

**Fat per muffin:** 2 grams

**Percent of calories from fat:** 14%

$W$e combined wheat bran with shredded carrots for a muffin rich in fiber and beta-carotene. The pineapple adds moistness and sunny sweetness.

1 cup unbleached all-purpose flour

½ cup wheat bran

2 teaspoons baking powder

½ teaspoon ground cinnamon

¼ teaspoon salt

1 large egg

½ cup packed brown sugar

1 tablespoon vegetable oil

½ cup skim milk

1 cup shredded carrots (1 to 2 carrots)

1 cup unsweetened crushed pineapple, drained after measuring

½ cup raisins

Preheat the oven to 400°F. Coat one 12- or two 6-muffin tins with nonstick cooking spray.

Whisk the flour with the bran, baking powder, cinnamon, and salt and set aside.

Beat the egg, brown sugar, and oil with an electric mixer set on high until smooth. Add the milk and beat again. Add the carrots, pineapple, and raisins and beat again. Mix the flour into the batter just until combined.

Spoon the batter into the muffin cups so that each is about two-thirds full. Bake for 20 to 25 minutes or until the muffins are lightly browned, puff up, and a toothpick inserted in the center comes out clean. Cool in the tin set on a wire rack for about 5 minutes. Remove the muffins from the tin and eat them warm, or let them cool completely on a wire rack.

In the bran muffin category, this is one of our all-time favorites. It is high in fiber and iron, and a world-class winner when it comes to flavor.

1¼ cups unbleached all-purpose flour
1 cup wheat bran
1½ teaspoons baking powder
1 large egg
¼ cup molasses
3 tablespoons packed brown sugar
2 tablespoons vegetable oil
1⅓ cups nonfat gelatin-free plain yogurt
½ cup raisins

Preheat the oven to 400°F. Coat one 12- or two 6-muffin tins with nonstick cooking spray.

Whisk the flour with the bran and baking powder and set aside.

Beat the egg, molasses, brown sugar, and oil with an electric mixer set on medium until smooth. Add the yogurt and beat again. Mix the flour and raisins into the batter by hand just until combined.

Spoon the batter into the muffin cups so that each is about two-thirds full. Bake for 15 to 20 minutes or until the muffins are lightly browned, puff up, and a toothpick inserted in the center comes out clean. Cool in the tin set on a wire rack for about 5 minutes. Remove the muffins from the tin and eat them warm, or let them cool completely on a wire rack.

# Raisin Bran Muffins

Yield: 12 muffins

Calories per muffin:
138

Fat per muffin:
3 grams

Percent of calories from fat:
20%

# Dr. Cookie's Seed Bran Muffins

**Yield:** 12 muffins

**Calories per muffin:** 155

**Fat per muffin:** 4 grams

**Percent of calories from fat:** 23%

These muffins are leavened with yeast, although they do not require kneading or much rising time. Be sure to mix the yeast with warm water, not hot, that is no more than 105°F. to 115°F. With the wheat bran, wheat germ, and seeds, the muffins pack a nutritional punch and are great for hiking or a picnic.

1 ¼-ounce package rapid-rise yeast (1 scant tablespoon)

½ cup warm water

¼ cup honey

2 large egg whites

¾ cup warm skim milk

¼ cup nonfat gelatin-free plain yogurt

2 tablespoons vegetable oil

1½ cups whole wheat flour

1 cup wheat bran

½ cup wheat germ

½ teaspoon ground cinnamon

½ teaspoon grated nutmeg

2 tablespoons poppy seeds

3 tablespoons millet seeds

½ cup raisins

Coat one 12- or two 6-muffin tins with nonstick cooking spray.

Sprinkle the yeast over the warm water and stir in 2 tablespoons honey. Let the mixture sit for about 5 minutes until it bubbles and foams.

Beat the egg whites with an electric mixer set on medium-high until foamy. Add the remaining 2 tablespoons honey, warm milk, yogurt, and oil and continue beating until smooth. Add the yeast mixture, the flour, wheat bran, wheat germ, cinnamon, nutmeg, poppy seeds, millet seeds, and raisins and mix by hand just until combined.

Spoon the batter into the muffin cups so that each is about two-thirds full. Cover the muffin tin with a kitchen towel and let sit for 20 minutes in a warm, draft-free place.

Preheat the oven to 350°F.

Bake the muffins for 15 to 20 minutes or until they are lightly browned, puff up, and feel firm. Cool in the tin set on a wire rack for about 5 minutes. Remove the muffins from the tin and eat them warm, or let them cool completely on a wire rack.

*The milk and the yogurt make the texture of muffins softer and more tender than usual. Try them for a change of pace—and a pretty good measure of calcium.*

   2  cups unbleached all-purpose flour
   ½  cup old-fashioned rolled oats
   1  teaspoon baking powder
   1  teaspoon baking soda
   ¼  teaspoon salt
   1  large egg
   ⅓  cup packed brown sugar
   2  tablespoons vegetable oil
   ¾  cup mashed ripe bananas (about 1½ bananas)
   ¼  cup skim milk
   ¾  cup nonfat gelatin-free plain yogurt
   1  teaspoon vanilla extract

Preheat the oven to 400°F. Coat one 12- or two 6-muffin tins with nonstick cooking spray.

Whisk the flour with the oats, baking powder, baking soda, and salt and set aside.

Beat the egg, brown sugar, and oil with an electric mixer set on medium until smooth. Add the bananas, milk, yogurt, and vanilla and beat again. Mix the flour into the batter by hand just until combined.

Spoon the batter into the muffin cups so that each is about two-thirds full. Bake for 15 to 18 minutes or until the muffins are lightly browned, puff up, and a toothpick inserted in the center comes out clean. Cool in the tin set on a wire rack for about 10 minutes. Remove the muffins from the tin and eat them warm, or let them cool completely on a wire rack.

# Banana-Oat Muffins

Yield: 12 muffins

Calories per muffin: 137

Fat per muffin: 3 grams

Percent of calories from fat: 20%

# Blueberry Muffins

Yield: 12 muffins

Calories per muffin: 170

Fat per muffin: 2.5 grams

Percent of calories from fat: 13%

**W**ho doesn't love blueberry muffins? They seem to welcome the day as few other baked goods do with their warmth and natural sweetness. However, blueberries are more than a wake-up call. They may help lower blood cholesterol. They contain as much pectin, a soluble fiber, as apples, pears, and peaches (although not as much as citrus fruit) and, like cranberries, may reduce recurrent urinary tract infections.

2 cups unbleached all-purpose flour

1 tablespoon baking powder

¼ teaspoon salt

1 large egg

1 cup sugar

2 tablespoons margarine, melted

1 cup skim milk

1 teaspoon vanilla extract

1½ cups fresh or frozen and thawed blueberries

Preheat the oven to 400°F. Coat one 12- or two 6-muffin tins with nonstick cooking spray.

Whisk the flour with the baking powder and salt and set aside.

Beat the egg, sugar, and margarine with an electric mixer set on medium until smooth. Add the milk and vanilla and beat again. Mix the flour and blueberries into the batter by hand just until combined.

Spoon the batter into the muffin cups so that each is about two-thirds full. Bake for 15 to 20 minutes or until the muffins are lightly browned, puff up, and a toothpick inserted in the center comes out clean. Cool in the tin set on a wire rack for about 10 minutes. Remove the muffins from the tin and eat them warm, or let them cool completely on a wire rack.

Anyone who has made cranberry sauce for the holidays knows what a perfect flavor combination cranberries and oranges are. Here, we combine the two in sweet, wonderful muffins that are great right from the oven but even better after sitting for a day or two.

2 cups unbleached all-purpose flour
1 tablespoon baking powder
¼ teaspoon salt
1 large egg
1 cup sugar
2 tablespoons margarine, melted
1 cup orange juice
1 teaspoon chopped orange peel
1¼ cups halved fresh or frozen and thawed cranberries

Preheat the oven to 400°F. Coat one 12- or two 6-muffin tins with nonstick cooking spray.

Whisk the flour with the baking powder and salt and set aside.

Beat the egg, sugar, and margarine with an electric mixer set on medium until smooth. Add the orange juice and orange peel and beat again. Mix the flour and cranberries into the batter by hand just until combined.

Spoon the batter into the muffin cups so that each is about two-thirds full. Bake for 15 to 20 minutes or until the muffins are lightly browned, puff up, and a toothpick inserted in the center comes out clean. Cool in the tin set on a wire rack for about 10 minutes. Remove the muffins from the tin and eat them warm, or let them cool completely on a wire rack.

# Cranberry Muffins

Yield: 12 muffins

Calories per muffin: 165

Fat per muffin: 2.6 grams

Percent of calories from fat: 14%

# Pumpkin-Cranberry Muffins

Yield: 12 muffins

Calories per muffin: 143

Fat per muffin: 3.1 grams

Percent of calories from fat: 20%

The combination of pumpkin puree and cranberries makes these a sure bet for autumn. Serve them for Thanksgiving breakfast or during the main event later in the day. Either way, they are lower in fat and calories than most Thanksgiving traditions and taste just as good.

2 cups unbleached all-purpose flour

1 tablespoon baking powder

1½ teaspoons pumpkin pie spice

1 large egg

½ cup packed brown sugar

2 tablespoons vegetable oil

1 cup unsweetened pumpkin puree

¼ cup nonfat gelatin-free plain yogurt

1½ cups fresh or frozen and thawed cranberries

Preheat the oven to 400°F. Coat one 12- or two 6-muffin tins with nonstick cooking spray.

Whisk the flour with the baking powder and pumpkin pie spice and set aside.

Beat the egg, brown sugar, and oil with an electric mixer set on medium until smooth. Add the pumpkin puree and yogurt and beat again. Mix the flour and cranberries into the batter by hand just until combined.

Spoon the batter into the muffin cups so that each is about two-thirds full. Bake for 15 to 20 minutes or until the muffins are lightly browned, puff up, and a toothpick inserted in the center comes out clean. Cool in the tin set on a wire rack for about 10 minutes. Remove the muffins from the tin and eat them warm, or let them cool completely on a wire rack.

$W_{e}$ bake the fruit into these muffins so there is no need for jam or marmalade, but if you want to spread a little "just-fruit" preserves on the warm-from-the-oven treats, by all means do so. Remember that apricots are a good source of potassium and magnesium, and they also are rich in beta-carotene—how can you go wrong?

1 cup unsweetened crushed pineapple, undrained
½ cup finely chopped dried apricots
2 cups unbleached all-purpose flour
2 teaspoons baking powder
½ teaspoon ground cinnamon
½ teaspoon grated nutmeg
½ teaspoon ground ginger
1 large egg
½ cup packed brown sugar
2 tablespoons vegetable oil
½ cup unsweetened pineapple juice

Preheat the oven to 400°F. Coat one 12- or two 6-muffin tins with nonstick cooking spray.

Mix the crushed pineapple with the dried apricots. Set aside.

Whisk the flour with the baking powder, cinnamon, nutmeg, and ginger and set aside.

Beat the egg, brown sugar, and oil with an electric mixer set on medium until smooth. Add the pineapple juice and beat again. Add the crushed pineapple and apricots and beat again. Mix the flour into the batter by hand just until combined.

Spoon the batter into the muffin cups so that each is about two-thirds full. Bake for 15 to 20 minutes or until the muffins are lightly browned, puff up, and a toothpick inserted in the center comes out clean. Cool in the tin set on a wire rack for about 10 minutes. Remove the muffins from the tin and eat them warm, or let them cool completely on a wire rack.

# Apricot-Pineapple Muffins

<u>Yield:</u> 12 muffins

<u>Calories per muffin:</u> 156

<u>Fat per muffin:</u> 3 grams

<u>Percent of calories from fat:</u> 17%

127

# Pumpkin-Pineapple Muffins

Yield: 12 muffins

Calories per muffin: 122

Fat per muffin: 3 grams

Percent of calories from fat: 22%

*These full-flavored muffins combine pineapple and pumpkin and a pinch of ginger to give their more subtle flavors zing.*

1 ½  cups unbleached all-purpose flour

1  teaspoon baking powder

1  teaspoon baking soda

½  teaspoon ground cinnamon

¼  teaspoon grated nutmeg

¼  teaspoon ground ginger

1  large egg

½  cup packed brown sugar

2  tablespoons vegetable oil

1  cup unsweetened pumpkin puree

½  cup unsweetened crushed pineapple, drained

Preheat the oven to 400°F. Coat one 12- or two 6-muffin tins with nonstick cooking spray.

Whisk the flour with the baking powder, baking soda, cinnamon, nutmeg, and ginger and set aside.

Beat the egg, brown sugar, and oil with an electric mixer set on medium until smooth. Add the pumpkin puree and pineapple and beat again. Mix the flour into the batter by hand just until combined.

Spoon the batter into the muffin cups so that each is about two-thirds full. Bake for 13 to 15 minutes or until the muffins are lightly browned, puff up, and a toothpick inserted in the center comes out clean. Cool in the tin set on a wire rack for about 10 minutes. Remove the muffins from the tin and eat them warm, or let them cool completely on a wire rack.

These sweet muffins are flavored with one of the most naturally sweet fruits available. Pineapples are a good source of vitamin C and the mineral manganese, which is important for strong bones and healthy connective tissues. The pineapple is also a symbol of welcome in America, a tradition dating back to New England's magnificent seafaring days. Make these luscious muffins the next time you welcome friends into your home for breakfast or brunch.

# Pineapple Muffins

Yield: 12 muffins

Calories per muffin: 163

Fat per muffin: 3 grams

Percent of calories from fat: 17%

2   cups unbleached all-purpose flour

2½  teaspoons baking powder

½   teaspoon baking soda

½   teaspoon ground ginger

1   large egg

½   cup packed brown sugar

2   tablespoons vegetable oil

1   cup unsweetened crushed pineapple, undrained

⅔   cup unsweetened pineapple or orange juice

¾   cup coarsely chopped dried pineapple

Preheat the oven to 400°F. Coat one 12- or two 6-muffin tins with nonstick cooking spray.

Whisk the flour with the baking powder, baking soda, and ginger and set aside.

Beat the egg, brown sugar, and oil with an electric mixer set on medium until smooth. Add the crushed pineapple, juice, and dried pineapple and beat again. Mix the flour into the batter by hand just until combined.

Spoon the batter into the muffin cups so that each is about two-thirds full. Bake for 15 to 20 minutes or until the muffins are lightly browned, puff up, and a toothpick inserted in the center comes out clean. Cool in the tin set on a wire rack for about 10 minutes. Remove the muffins from the tin and eat them warm, or let them cool completely on a wire rack.

# Dried Fruit Muffins

**Yield:** 12 muffins

**Calories per muffin:** 163

**Fat per muffin:** 3 grams

**Percent of calories from fat:** 17%

**W**e remember when dried fruits meant raisins, prunes, and maybe apricots. Times have changed. Now when we go to the store, we see more and more variety in the dried fruit section. Many of the fruits are dried with little or no added sugar, which we think is just terrific. When the fruits are dehydrated their natural sweetness intensifies and there is no reason to add sugar. For this recipe we use a snack-pack available in our local market that includes dried cherries, cranberries, apricots, apples, and raisins. Even better, the fruit is already cut up! Experiment with your own favorite combinations. If the market near you is weak in the dried fruit department, try the nearest natural foods store. And if the fruits are too sticky to cut up easily, toss them with a little of the flour.

1 cup unbleached all-purpose flour

1 cup quick-cooking oats (not instant)

3 teaspoons baking powder

½ teaspoon grated nutmeg

½ teaspoon ground cinnamon

¼ teaspoon salt

1 large egg, at room temperature

⅓ cup packed brown sugar

⅓ cup granulated sugar

2 tablespoons vegetable oil

1 cup skim milk, at room temperature

¾ cup chopped mixed dried fruit, such as cherries, cranberries, raisins, apples

Preheat the oven to 400°F. Coat one 12- or two 6-muffin tins with nonstick cooking spray.

Whisk the flour with the oats, baking powder, nutmeg, cinnamon, and salt and set aside.

Beat the egg, sugars, and oil with an electric mixer set on medium until smooth. Add the milk and beat again. Mix the flour and dried fruit into the batter by hand just until combined.

Spoon the batter into the muffin cups so that each is about two-thirds full. Bake for 15 to 20 minutes or until the muffins are lightly browned, puff up, and a toothpick inserted in the center comes out clean. Cool in the tin set on a wire rack for about 10 minutes. Remove the muffins from the tin and eat them warm, or let them cool completely on a wire rack.

W*e add orange juice to the oats for a jolt of flavor and a dose of vitamin C. The oats provide nutty flavor and a lot of valuable fiber. Be sure they absorb all the liquid before stirring them into the batter.*

    1  cup old-fashioned rolled oats
    ½  cup boiling water
    ½  cup orange juice
    1  cup unbleached all-purpose flour
    2  teaspoons baking powder
    ½  teaspoon baking soda
    ¼  teaspoon salt
    1  large egg
    ⅓  cup packed brown sugar
    ⅓  cup granulated sugar
    2  tablespoons vegetable oil
    1  teaspoon grated orange rind
    ½  cup golden raisins

Preheat the oven to 400°F. Coat one 12- or two 6-muffin tins with nonstick cooking spray.

Stir the oats into the boiling water. Add the orange juice and stir again. Set aside.

Whisk the flour with the baking powder, baking soda, and salt and set aside.

Beat the egg, sugars, and oil with an electric mixer set on medium until smooth. Add the oats and orange rind and beat again. Mix the flour and raisins into the batter by hand just until combined.

Spoon the batter into the muffin cups so that each is about two-thirds full. Bake for 15 to 18 minutes or until the muffins are lightly browned, puff up, and a toothpick inserted in the center comes out clean. Cool in the tin set on a wire rack for about 10 minutes. Remove the muffins from the tin and eat them warm, or let them cool completely on a wire rack.

# Oatmeal-Orange Muffins

Yield: 12 muffins

Calories per muffin: 151

Fat per muffin: 3 grams

Percent of calories from fat: 18%

# Whole Wheat Cinnamon-Raisin Muffins

Yield: 12 muffins

Calories per muffin: 147

Fat per muffin: 3.3 grams

Percent of calories from fat: 20%

*Whole wheat flour contains the bran, endosperm, and germ of the wheat, which makes it more nutritious than all-purpose white flour, which has been stripped of all but the starchy endosperm. But because of this, whole wheat flour is heavier than all-purpose. This is why we combine the two. If we used only whole wheat, even these yummy muffins would be heavy and unappealing.*

1 cup unbleached all-purpose flour

¾ cup whole wheat flour

2 teaspoons baking powder

½ teaspoon baking soda

1½ teaspoons ground cinnamon

1 large egg

½ cup packed brown sugar

2 tablespoons vegetable oil

1 cup plus 2 tablespoons buttermilk

½ cup raisins

Preheat the oven to 400°F. Coat one 12- or two 6-muffin tins with nonstick cooking spray.

Whisk the flours with the baking powder, baking soda, and cinnamon and set aside.

Beat the egg, brown sugar, and oil with an electric mixer set on medium until smooth. Add the buttermilk and beat again. Mix the flour and raisins into the batter by hand just until combined.

Spoon the batter into the muffin cups so that each is about two-thirds full. Bake for 15 to 20 minutes or until the muffins are lightly browned, puff up, and a toothpick inserted in the center comes out clean. Cool in the tin set on a wire rack for about 10 minutes. Remove the muffins from the tin and eat them warm, or let them cool completely on a wire rack.

We really like the hint of maple flavor in these muffins. It mingles seductively with the walnuts to make these just the thing to warm up a blustery day. We admit the muffins fall into the "splurge" category, as the percent of calories from fat is higher than our 30 percent limit. But what the heck? They're worth it every now and then. (And the fat grams—not percent—is what really counts!)

1 cup wheat bran

1 cup boiling water

1 cup unbleached all-purpose flour

2 teaspoons baking powder

½ teaspoon baking soda

1 large egg

½ cup packed brown sugar

2 tablespoons vegetable oil

½ cup nonfat gelatin-free plain yogurt

1½ teaspoons maple extract

½ cup raisins

¼ cup chopped walnuts

Preheat the oven to 400°F. Coat one 12- or two 6-muffin tins with nonstick cooking spray.

Stir the wheat bran into the boiling water and set aside.

Whisk the flour with the baking powder and baking soda and set aside.

Beat the egg, brown sugar, and oil with an electric mixer set on medium until smooth. Add the wheat bran, yogurt, and maple extract and beat again. Mix the flour, raisins, and nuts into the batter by hand just until combined.

Spoon the batter into the muffin cups so that each is about two-thirds full. Bake for 15 to 20 minutes or until the muffins are lightly browned, puff up, and a toothpick inserted in the center comes out clean. Cool in the tin set on a wire rack for about 10 minutes. Remove the muffins from the tin and eat them warm, or let them cool completely on a wire rack.

# Maple-Walnut Muffins

Yield: 12 muffins

Calories per muffin: 124

Fat per muffin: 4.6 grams

Percent of calories from fat: 33%

133

Muffins and Biscuits

# Curried Rice and Raisin Muffins

Yield: 12 muffins

Calories per muffin: 102

Fat per muffin: 1.8 grams

Percent of calories from fat: 16%

*T*hese aren't breakfast muffins. They are meant to be eaten a little later in the day. We especially like them with spinach salad tossed with a curry dressing, and they are great with vegetable soup, too. We suggest you vary the amount of curry powder by ¼ teaspoon or so depending on your own taste and the strength of the particular spice mixture. Brown rice is more nutritious than white rice and gives these muffins a distinctive nutty flavor.

1¼ cups unbleached all-purpose flour

2 teaspoons baking powder

1 teaspoon curry powder, approximately

¼ teaspoon salt

1 large egg

2 tablespoons packed brown sugar

1 tablespoon vegetable oil

1 cup cooked brown rice

½ cup raisins

Preheat the oven to 400°F. Coat one 12- or two 6-muffin tins with nonstick cooking spray.

Whisk the flour with the baking powder, curry powder, and salt and set aside.

Beat the egg, brown sugar, and oil with an electric mixer set on medium until smooth. Add the rice and beat again. Mix the flour and raisins into the batter by hand just until combined.

Spoon the batter into the muffin cups so that each is about two-thirds full. Bake for 15 to 17 minutes or until the muffins are lightly browned, puff up, and a toothpick inserted in the center comes out clean. Cool in the tin set on a wire rack for about 10 minutes. Remove the muffins from the tin and eat them warm, or let them cool completely on a wire rack.

_ossing a handful of poppy seeds into the muffin batter results in a mildly flavored bread with a slight crunch._

2 cups unbleached all-purpose flour
2 teaspoons baking powder
¼ teaspoon salt
3 tablespoons poppy seeds
1 large egg
1 large egg white
¾ cup sugar
2 tablespoons vegetable oil
¾ cup orange juice
1 tablespoon grated orange rind

Preheat the oven to 400°F. Coat one 12- or two 6-muffin tins with nonstick cooking spray.

Whisk the flour with the baking powder, salt, and poppy seeds and set aside.

Beat the egg, egg white, sugar, and oil with an electric mixer set on medium until smooth. Add the orange juice and orange rind and beat again. Mix the flour into the batter by hand just until combined.

Spoon the batter into the muffin cups so that each is about two-thirds full. Bake for 15 to 20 minutes or until the muffins are lightly browned, puff up, and a toothpick inserted in the center comes out clean. Cool in the tin set on a wire rack for about 10 minutes. Remove the muffins from the tin and eat them warm, or let them cool completely on a wire rack.

# Poppy Seed Muffins

Yield: 12 muffins

Calories per muffin: 161

Fat per muffin: 4 grams

Percent of calories from fat: 22%

# Sweet Potato Muffins

**Yield:** 12 muffins

**Calories per muffin:**
165 without pecans; 182 with pecans

**Fat per muffin:**
3 grams without pecans; 4.7 grams with pecans

**Percent of calories from fat:**
16% without pecans; 23% with pecans

*Sweet potatoes are the granddaddies of vitamin A. One cup has more beta-carotene (which the body converts to vitamin A) than a cup of carrots. They're also moist, sweet, and delicious. If fat and calories are not a major concern, they marry extremely well with pecans.*

2 cups unbleached all-purpose flour

2½ teaspoons baking powder

½ teaspoon baking soda

1 teaspoon ground cinnamon

¼ teaspoon grated nutmeg

¼ teaspoon ground ginger

¼ teaspoon ground allspice

¼ teaspoon ground cloves

1 large egg

½ cup packed brown sugar

2 tablespoons vegetable oil

1 cup orange juice

1 teaspoon vanilla extract

1 cup mashed cooked sweet potato (about 12 ounces of potato)

¼ cup chopped pecans (optional)

Preheat the oven to 400°F. Coat one 12- or two 6-muffin tins with nonstick cooking spray.

Whisk the flour with the baking powder, baking soda, cinnamon, nutmeg, ginger, allspice, and cloves and set aside.

Beat the egg, brown sugar, and oil with an electric mixer set on medium until smooth. Add the orange juice, vanilla, and sweet potato and beat again. Mix the flour and pecans, if desired, into the batter by hand just until combined.

Spoon the batter into the muffin cups so that each is about two-thirds full. Bake for 15 to 20 minutes or until the muffins are lightly browned, puff up, and a toothpick inserted in the center comes out clean. Cool in the tin set on a wire rack for about 10 minutes. Remove the muffins from the tin and eat them warm, or let them cool completely on a wire rack.

As promised on page 79 in the recipe for *Whole Wheat Zucchini Cake*, we have developed a number of recipes for coping with the annual autumn zucchini invasion. These muffins, bolstered by a cup of shredded zucchini, are lusciously moist and tasty. The whole wheat flour provides a little nuttiness to perk up the admittedly bland zucchini. The walnuts add even more flavor—and also more fat.

1 ½ cups unbleached all-purpose flour

½ cup whole wheat flour

2 teaspoons baking powder

½ teaspoon ground cinnamon

¼ teaspoon grated nutmeg

¼ teaspoon ground ginger

1 large egg

⅔ cup packed brown sugar

2 tablespoons vegetable oil

1 cup orange juice

1 teaspoon vanilla extract

1 cup shredded zucchini (about 1 to 2 medium zucchini)

½ cup raisins

¼ cup chopped walnuts (optional)

Preheat the oven to 400°F. Coat one 12- or two 6-muffin tins with nonstick cooking spray.

Whisk the flours with the baking powder, cinnamon, nutmeg, and ginger and set aside.

Beat the egg, brown sugar, and oil with an electric mixer set on medium until smooth. Add the orange juice and vanilla and beat again. Mix the flour, zucchini, raisins, and walnuts, if desired, into the batter by hand just until combined.

Spoon the batter into the muffin cups so that each is about two-thirds full. Bake for 15 to 20 minutes or until the muffins are lightly browned, puff up, and a toothpick inserted in the center comes out clean. Cool in the tin set on a wire rack for about 10 minutes. Remove the muffins from the tin and eat them warm, or let them cool completely on a wire rack.

# Zucchini Muffins

Yield: 12 muffins

Calories per muffin:
167 without walnuts; 183 with walnuts

Fat per muffin:
3 grams without walnuts; 4.5 grams with walnuts

Percent of calories from fat:
16% without walnuts; 22% with walnuts

137

Muffins and Biscuits

# Cornmeal Muffins

**Yield:** 12 muffins

**Calories per muffin:** 113

**Fat per muffin:** 2.3 grams

**Percent of calories from fat:** 18%

*Cornmeal is made by grinding up corn; corn flour is made by grinding the meal even finer. We love the natural sweetness and distinctive crumbly texture of baked goods made with cornmeal. These muffins are no exception. We combine the cornmeal with all-purpose flour to help leaven and lighten the muffins.*

1 cup unbleached all-purpose flour
1 cup yellow cornmeal
1 teaspoon baking powder
1 teaspoon baking soda
¼ teaspoon salt
1 large egg
¼ cup honey
1 tablespoon vegetable oil
1 cup buttermilk

Preheat the oven to 400°F. Coat one 12- or two 6-muffin tins with nonstick cooking spray.

Whisk the flour with the cornmeal, baking powder, baking soda, and salt and set aside.

Beat the egg, honey, and oil with an electric mixer set on medium until smooth. Add the buttermilk and beat again. Mix the flour into the batter by hand just until combined.

Spoon the batter into the muffin cups so that each is about two-thirds full. Bake for about 15 minutes or until the muffins are lightly browned, puff up, and a toothpick inserted in the center comes out clean. Cool in the tin set on a wire rack for about 10 minutes. Remove the muffins from the tin and eat them warm, or let them cool completely on a wire rack.

**B**ecause so many of us need a chocolate fix every now and then, we developed these lovely muffins. Some may prefer to call them cupcakes, since they seem more like dessert than breakfast or snack fare. It doesn't matter what you call them—one bite and you're sure to love them.

2 cups unbleached all-purpose flour

3 teaspoons baking powder

¼ teaspoon salt

1 large egg

1 cup sugar

2 tablespoons margarine, melted

1 cup skim milk

1 teaspoon vanilla extract

⅓ cup mini semisweet chocolate chips

Preheat the oven to 400°F. Coat one 12- or two 6-muffin tins with nonstick cooking spray.

Whisk the flour with the baking powder and salt and set aside.

Beat the egg, sugar, and margarine with an electric mixer set on medium until smooth. Add the milk and vanilla and beat again. Mix the flour and chocolate chips into the batter by hand just until combined.

Spoon the batter into the muffin cups so that each is about two-thirds full. Bake for about 15 minutes or until the muffins are lightly browned, puff up, and a toothpick inserted in the center comes out clean. Cool in the tin set on a wire rack for about 10 minutes. Remove the muffins from the tin and eat them warm, or let them cool completely on a wire rack.

# Chocolate Chip Muffins

Yield: 12 muffins

Calories per muffin: 194

Fat per muffin: 3.8 grams

Percent of calories from fat: 18%

# Buttermilk Biscuits

**Yield:** 10 biscuits

**Calories per biscuit:** 129

**Fat per biscuit:** 4 grams

**Percent of calories from fat:** 28%

*These biscuits have just enough fat to make them light and tender. We set out to make nonfat biscuits, but abandoned the idea when we discovered they were even harder to eat than to make! These are drop biscuits and so are unevenly shaped. Split them open and spread the hot biscuits with strawberry or blueberry "just-fruit" preserves. Or use them for shortcake.*

    2  cups unbleached all-purpose flour
    2  teaspoons baking powder
    ¼  teaspoon baking soda
    ¼  teaspoon salt
    1  tablespoon sugar
    3  tablespoons cold margarine, cut into ½-inch pieces
    1  cup plus 2 tablespoons buttermilk

Preheat the oven to 425°F. Coat a baking sheet with nonstick cooking spray.

Put the flour, baking powder, baking soda, salt, and sugar into the bowl of a food processor fitted with the metal blade. Process for about 2 seconds. Drop the margarine pieces on top of the flour and process for about 8 seconds. The mixture will be the consistency of coarse crumbs. Do not overprocess. Transfer the mixture to a mixing bowl. Alternatively, cut the margarine into the flour using a pastry blade, 2 forks, or your fingertips.

Stir the buttermilk into the dry ingredients with a fork just until combined. When the biscuit dough holds together, drop it by large spoonfuls onto the baking sheet.

Bake for 10 to 12 minutes or until the biscuits are puffy and lightly browned. Serve them immediately.

These biscuits are similar to the Buttermilk Biscuits on page 140, but because they contain multigrain cereal, raisins, and apple, have more texture and lots more fiber. They are also more robust and make a great midday snack or accompaniment to a light meal.

1 cup unbleached all-purpose flour

1 tablespoon baking powder

1 teaspoon ground cinnamon

¼ teaspoon salt

2 tablespoons packed brown sugar

3 tablespoons cold margarine, cut into ½-inch pieces

1 large egg

⅓ cup skim milk

1 cup quick-cooking multigrain cereal, such as Quaker, or quick-cooking oats (not instant)

¼ cup raisins

¼ cup finely chopped unpeeled apple

Preheat the oven to 425°F. Coat a baking sheet with nonstick cooking spray.

Put the flour, baking powder, cinnamon, salt, and brown sugar into the bowl of a food processor fitted with the metal blade. Process for about 2 seconds. Drop the margarine pieces on top of the flour and process for about 8 seconds. The mixture will be the consistency of coarse crumbs. Do not overprocess. Transfer the mixture to a mixing bowl. Alternatively, cut the margarine into the flour using a pastry blade, 2 forks, or your fingertips.

Whisk the egg and milk together. Stir the cereal into the mixture. Add the flour, raisins, and apple and stir with a fork until combined. When the biscuit dough holds together, drop it by large spoonfuls onto the baking sheet.

Bake for 10 to 12 minutes or until the biscuits are puffy and lightly browned. Serve them immediately.

# Multigrain Biscuits

**Yield:** 10 biscuits

**Calories per biscuit:** 135

**Fat per biscuit:** 4.3 grams

**Percent of calories from fat:** 30%

# Potato-Dill Biscuits

**Yield:** 12 biscuits

**Calories per biscuit:** 100

**Fat per biscuit:** 1.3 grams

**Percent of calories from fat:** 12%

*W*e love how the flavor of dill shines through in these potato biscuits. If you use leftover mashed potatoes that were salted when originally made, omit the salt from the recipe.

2 cups unbleached all-purpose flour

2 teaspoons baking powder

½ teaspoon baking soda

¼ teaspoon salt

1 teaspoon dried dill

2 teaspoons dillseed

1 tablespoon sugar

¾ cup skim milk

1 tablespoon melted and cooled margarine

1 cup mashed cooked potato (about 12 ounces of potato)

Preheat the oven to 425°F. Coat a baking sheet with nonstick cooking spray.

Whisk the flour with the baking powder, baking soda, salt, dill and dillseed, and sugar and set aside.

Beat the milk, margarine, and potato with an electric mixer set on medium until smooth. Stir the flour into the dough just until combined. When the biscuit dough holds together, drop it by large spoonfuls onto the baking sheet.

Bake for about 15 minutes or until the biscuits are puffy, lightly browned, and a toothpick inserted in the center of one comes out clean. Serve them immediately.

## Chapter 6

# Quick Breads

If zucchini and banana bread jump to mind when you consider quick breads, you won't be disappointed with our recipes. But we go beyond the expected and include recipes for nut-free date-nut bread, spicy corn bread, and an intoxicating plum bread you'll be wild about, to name just a few.

Traditional quick bread loaves contain as much as a cup of oil or margarine. That's more fat than any self-respecting bread (or bread lover) needs! We cut back the oil to one or two tablespoons in many loaves, and some breads are totally fat-free. To lighten them, we added nonfat yogurt, applesauce, or a similar nonfat ingredient. Our kitchens were redolent with the heady aromas of baking bread as we experimented, looking for the right combination of low-fat, low-calorie, and high-flavor ingredients. When we add nuts to a bread—and some quick breads beg for their crunch—we do so moderately. No one disputes the nutritional value of nuts, but they are super fattening. We computed the calories and fat based on getting 14 slices of bread from one loaf. If you slice it thinner, the counts will be slightly lower; fatter slices have higher counts.

Read the instructions for mixing muffin batters (page 116) before making the quick breads. The same general guidelines apply about combining wet and dry ingredients and taking care not to overmix.

Finally, low-fat breads turn stale sooner than others. Or so we have heard; none lasts long enough in our houses to test the theory!

Throughout the book we call for unpeeled apples. The whole apple, skin and all, is a neat, healthful package that provides pectin, an important fiber that has been shown to lower LDL cholesterol levels, while raising HDL cholesterol levels. And that's good! It's a great idea to eat a few raw apples every day, if you can, but eating a slice or two of this apple-packed bread is good for you, too. And it tastes wonderful. Can you beat it?

    2  cups unbleached all-purpose flour
    1  teaspoon baking powder
    1  teaspoon baking soda
    1  teaspoon ground cinnamon
    ¼  teaspoon salt
    1  large egg
    2  large egg whites
    ⅔  cup packed brown sugar
    ½  cup natural unsweetened applesauce
    1½ cups shredded unpeeled apples (about 2 apples)
    ¾  cup raisins

Preheat the oven to 350°F. Coat a 9-by-5-inch loaf pan with nonstick cooking spray.

Whisk the flour with the baking powder, baking soda, cinnamon, and salt and set aside.

Beat the egg, egg whites, and brown sugar with an electric mixer set at medium until smooth. Add the applesauce and beat again. Stir the flour, shredded apples, and raisins into the batter by hand just until combined.

Scrape the batter into the prepared pan. Bake for 40 to 45 minutes or until a toothpick inserted in the center of the loaf comes out clean. The crust may crack. Cool the bread in the pan set on a wire rack for about 10 minutes. Turn out onto a wire rack and cool completely.

# Double Apple Bread

Yield: 1 loaf; 14 slices

Calories per slice: 140

Fat per slice: .8 gram

Percent of calories from fat: 5%

# Apple Pie Bread

**Yield:** I loaf; 14 slices

**Calories per slice:** 158

**Fat per slice:** 2 grams

**Percent of calories from fat:** 12%

The chunks of apple and the hint of cinnamon make us think of apple pie. But the bread has less fat and far fewer calories per slice than most pies. Indulge!

 2  cups unbleached all-purpose flour
 ½ cup old-fashioned rolled oats
 1  teaspoon baking powder
 1  teaspoon baking soda
 1  teaspoon ground cinnamon
 ¼ teaspoon salt
 1  large egg
 1  large egg white
 ½ cup packed brown sugar
 ¼ cup honey
 1  tablespoon vegetable oil
 1  cup buttermilk
 1¼ cups finely chopped unpeeled apples (about 1 to 2 apples)

Preheat the oven to 350°F. Coat a 9-by-5-inch loaf pan with nonstick cooking spray.

Whisk the flour with the oats, baking powder, baking soda, cinnamon, and salt and set aside.

Beat the egg, egg white, brown sugar, honey, and oil with an electric mixer set at medium until smooth. Add the buttermilk and beat again. Stir the flour and apples into the batter by hand just until combined.

Scrape the batter into the prepared pan. Bake for 50 to 60 minutes or until a toothpick inserted in the center of the loaf comes out clean. The crust may crack. Cool the bread in the pan set on a wire rack for about 10 minutes. Turn out onto a wire rack and cool completely.

The grated apple enhances this mild gingerbread, underscoring its flavor and moistening it at the same time.

2 cups unbleached all-purpose flour
1½ teaspoons baking powder
1 teaspoon baking soda
1½ teaspoons ground ginger
¼ teaspoon salt
1 large egg
2 large egg whites
½ cup packed brown sugar
⅓ cup molasses
2 tablespoons vegetable oil
½ cup buttermilk
1 cup grated unpeeled apple (about 1 apple)

Preheat the oven to 350°F. Coat a 9-by-5-inch loaf pan with nonstick cooking spray.

Whisk the flour with the baking powder, baking soda, ginger, and salt and set aside.

Beat the egg, egg whites, brown sugar, molasses, and oil with an electric mixer set at medium until smooth. Add the buttermilk and beat again. Stir the flour and apple into the batter by hand just until combined.

Scrape the batter into the prepared pan. Bake for 50 to 60 minutes or until a toothpick inserted in the center of the loaf comes out clean. The crust may crack. Cool the bread in the pan set on a wire rack for about 10 minutes. Turn out onto a wire rack and cool completely.

# Gingerbread with Apple

Yield: 1 loaf; 14 slices

Calories per slice: 141

Fat per slice: 2.7 grams

Percent of calories from fat: 17%

# Almost Perfect Pear Bread

**Yield:** 1 loaf; 14 slices

**Calories per slice:** 180

**Fat per slice:** 4 grams

**Percent of calories from fat:** 20%

**P**ears release relatively copious amounts of liquid as they cook, so making "perfect" pear bread is not always possible. This comes close, and depending on the juiciness of the pears, this will be the best pear bread you ever put in your mouth. We suggest adding a few more teaspoons of applesauce if the pears are not juicy. And don't panic if the batter seems on the dry side; it's supposed to be.

  2  cups unbleached all-purpose flour
  1  teaspoon baking powder
  1  teaspoon baking soda
  1  teaspoon ground cinnamon
  ½  teaspoon ground cloves
  ¼  teaspoon salt
  1  large egg
  2  large egg whites
  ½  cup packed brown sugar
  2  tablespoons vegetable oil
  ¼  cup honey
  3  tablespoons natural unsweetened applesauce, approximately
  1  teaspoon grated lemon rind
  1  cup finely chopped unpeeled pear (about 1 pear)
  ¾  cup raisins

Preheat the oven to 350°F. Coat a 9-by-5-inch loaf pan with nonstick cooking spray.

Whisk the flour with the baking powder, baking soda, cinnamon, cloves, and salt and set aside.

Beat the egg, egg whites, brown sugar, and oil with an electric mixer set at medium until smooth. Add the honey, applesauce, and lemon rind and beat again. Stir the flour, pear, and raisins into the batter by hand just until combined.

Scrape the batter into the prepared pan. Bake for 40 to 50 minutes or until a toothpick inserted in the center of the loaf comes out clean. The crust may crack. Cool the bread in the pan set on a wire rack for about 10 minutes. Turn out onto a wire rack and cool completely.

In previous chapters we extoll the virtues of blueberries. Like apples, they contain a terrific amount of pectin and may help lower blood cholesterol; like cranberries they may eliminate some of the symptoms of urinary tract infections. They also taste very, very good and we urge you to use them in baked goods as often as possible. Buy them in the summer when they are plump and sweet, and make bread and muffins often. Freeze the summer crop for use all through the year or look for unsweetened frozen blueberries in the market. This bread is great with blueberries, but tastes equally good with cranberries—or a combination of the two.

2½ cups unbleached all-purpose flour

1 tablespoon baking powder

1 large egg

1 large egg white

¾ cup sugar

2 tablespoons margarine, melted and cooled

1 cup skim milk

2 teaspoons grated lemon or orange rind

2 cup fresh or frozen and thawed blueberries

Preheat the oven to 350°F. Coat a 9-by-5-inch loaf pan with nonstick cooking spray.

Whisk the flour with the baking powder and set aside.

Beat the egg, egg white, sugar, and margarine with an electric mixer set at medium until smooth. Add the milk and lemon or orange rind and beat again. Stir the flour and blueberries into the batter by hand just until combined.

Scrape the batter into the prepared pan. Bake for 50 to 60 minutes or until a toothpick inserted in the center of the loaf comes out clean. The crust may crack. Cool the bread in the pan set on a wire rack for about 10 minutes. Turn out onto a wire rack and cool completely.

# Blueberry Bread

Yield: 1 loaf; 14 slices

Calories per slice: 146

Fat per slice: 2.3 grams

Percent of calories from fat: 14%

# Cranberry-Raisin Bread

Yield: 1 loaf; 14 slices

Calories per slice: 158

Fat per slice: 3.6 grams

Percent of calories from fat: 21%

W e often take samples of our recipes to the hospital for unbiased taste-testing. The doctors, nurses, and everyone else on staff are always honest and helpful, offering comments that generally find their way back to our kitchens (or drawing boards, as it were). Therefore, we were gratified when a nurse we admire very much generously gave us this fantastic recipe.

  2 cups unbleached all-purpose flour
  2 teaspoons baking powder
  1 teaspoon ground cinnamon
  ½ teaspoon grated nutmeg
  ½ teaspoon ground cloves
  1 large egg
  ½ cup honey
  2 tablespoons vegetable oil
  ½ cup orange juice
  1 teaspoon grated orange rind
  1½ cups chopped fresh or frozen and thawed cranberries
  ½ cup golden raisins
  ¼ cup chopped walnuts

Preheat the oven to 350°F. Coat a 9-by-5-inch loaf pan with nonstick cooking spray.

Whisk the flour with the baking powder, cinnamon, nutmeg, and cloves and set aside.

Beat the egg, honey, and oil with an electric mixer set at high until smooth. Add the orange juice and orange rind and beat again. Stir the flour, cranberries, raisins, and walnuts into the batter by hand just until combined.

Scrape the batter into the prepared pan. Bake for 50 to 60 minutes or until a toothpick inserted in the center of the loaf comes out clean. The crust may crack. Cool the bread in the pan set on a wire rack for about 10 minutes. Turn out onto a wire rack and cool completely.

**C**ranberries and orange are a traditional flavor combination for a very good reason. They taste wonderful together. Fresh cranberries are available only in late fall, so we often make lots of cranberry bread then. But if you freeze the fresh berries, you can have this wonderful, simple bread any time. If you use frozen berries, no need to thaw them before mixing them in the batter.

1½ cups unbleached all-purpose flour
1 tablespoon baking powder
½ teaspoon baking soda
¼ teaspoon salt
1 large egg
1 large egg white
1 cup sugar
2 tablespoons vegetable oil
1 cup orange juice
1 teaspoon grated orange rind
1½ cup fresh or frozen cranberries

Preheat the oven to 350°F. Coat a 9-by-5-inch loaf pan with nonstick cooking spray.

Whisk the flour with the baking powder, baking soda, and salt and set aside.

Beat the egg, egg white, sugar, and oil with an electric mixer set at medium until smooth. Add the orange juice and orange rind and beat again. Stir the flour and cranberries into the batter by hand just until combined.

Scrape the batter into the prepared pan. Bake for 50 to 60 minutes or until a toothpick inserted in the center of the loaf comes out clean. The crust may crack. Cool the bread in the pan set on a wire rack for about 10 minutes. Turn out onto a wire rack and cool completely.

# Cranberry-Orange Bread

Yield: 1 loaf; 14 slices

Calories per slice: 145

Fat per slice: 2.6 grams

Percent of calories from fat: 16%

# Pumpkin-Cranberry Bread

Yield: I loaf; 14 slices

Calories per slice:
155 without walnuts; 167 with walnuts

Fat per slice:
2.6 grams without walnuts; 3.9 grams with walnuts

Percent of calories from fat:
15% without walnuts; 21% with walnuts

Perhaps it's ridiculously obvious, but we love cranberry bread. We also think canned pumpkin puree is one of the best ingredients going. It's easy to find in the markets and adds subtle flavor, pleasing moistness, and plenty of vitamins to quick breads. Make sure you don't mistakenly buy pumpkin pie filling, which is sweetened.

2 cups unbleached all-purpose flour
½ teaspoon baking powder
1 teaspoon baking soda
½ teaspoon ground cinnamon
½ teaspoon grated nutmeg
½ teaspoon ground ginger
¼ teaspoon ground cloves
1 large egg
2 large egg whites
½ cup packed brown sugar
¼ cup granulated sugar
2 tablespoons vegetable oil
⅓ cup orange juice
1 cup unsweetened pumpkin puree
1 cup fresh or frozen and thawed cranberries
½ raisins
¼ cup chopped walnuts (optional)

Preheat the oven to 350°F. Coat a 9-by-5-inch loaf pan with nonstick cooking spray.

Whisk the flour with the baking powder, baking soda, cinnamon, nutmeg, ginger, and cloves and set aside.

Beat the egg, egg whites, sugars, and oil with an electric mixer set at medium until smooth. Add the orange juice and pumpkin and beat again. Stir the flour mixture, cranberries, raisins, and walnuts, if desired, into the batter by hand just until combined.

Scrape the batter into the prepared pan. Bake for 50 to 55 minutes or until a toothpick inserted in the center of the loaf comes out clean. The crust may crack. Cool the bread in the pan set on a wire rack for about 10 minutes. Turn out onto a wire rack and cool completely.

We consider this bread a dietary fiber champ. It's packed with whole-grain flour, bran, and lots of good-tasting dried fruit. The yogurt keeps it tender and moist. Go for it!

1 cup plus 1 tablespoon unbleached all-purpose flour

1 cup whole wheat flour

½ cup wheat bran

1 teaspoon baking powder

1 teaspoon baking soda

¼ teaspoon salt

1 cup chopped mixed dried fruit, such as apricots, apples, pineapple, raisins

2 large egg whites

¼ cup packed brown sugar

¼ cup honey

2 tablespoons vegetable oil

1½ cups nonfat gelatin-free plain yogurt

1 teaspoon grated orange rind

½ cup chopped pitted prunes

Preheat the oven to 350°F. Coat a 9-by-5-inch loaf pan with nonstick cooking spray.

Whisk 1 cup all-purpose flour with the whole wheat flour, bran, baking powder, baking soda, and salt and set aside.

Toss the mixed fruit with the remaining tablespoon flour and set aside.

Beat the egg whites, brown sugar, honey, and oil with an electric mixer set at high until smooth. Add the yogurt and orange rind and beat again. Stir the flour, prunes, and mixed fruit into the batter by hand just until combined.

Scrape the batter into the prepared pan. Bake for 50 to 60 minutes or until a toothpick inserted in the center of the loaf comes out clean. The crust may crack. Cool the bread in the pan set on a wire rack for about 10 minutes. Turn out onto a wire rack and cool completely.

# Yogurt Fruit Bread

Yield: 1 loaf; 14 slices

Calories per slice:
166, approximately, depending on selection of fruit

Fat per slice: 2.5 grams

Percent of calories from fat: 14%

# Dried Fruit Potato Bread

**Yield:** 1 loaf; 14 slices

**Calories per slice:**
165 without nuts;
178 with nuts

**Fat per slice:**
2.6 grams without nuts;
3.9 grams with nuts

**Percent of calories from fat:**
14% without nuts;
20% with nuts

Cooked potato adds significant moistness to the bread. Use leftover mashed potatoes (as long as they contain no salt or fats such as butter or cream) or mash a cooked potato or two with a fork or potato masher. Although we generally suggest leaving the skin on whole fruits and vegetables, in this case, the bread looks a lot more appetizing if the potato is peeled before mashing.

2 cups unbleached all-purpose flour

2 teaspoons baking powder

1 teaspoon baking soda

½ teaspoon ground cinnamon

½ teaspoon grated nutmeg

½ teaspoon ground allspice

½ teaspoon ground ginger

1 large egg

1 large egg white

¾ cup sugar

2 tablespoons vegetable oil

¾ cup mashed cooked potato

¾ cup skim milk

½ cup raisins

½ cup mixed candied fruits (fruitcake mix)

¼ cup chopped nuts, such as walnuts, pecans, or almonds (optional)

Preheat the oven to 350°F. Coat a 9-by-5-inch loaf pan with nonstick cooking spray.

Whisk the flour with the baking powder, baking soda, cinnamon, nutmeg, allspice, and ginger and set aside.

Beat the egg, egg white, sugar, and oil with an electric mixer set at medium until smooth. Add the mashed potato and milk and beat again. Stir the flour, raisins, fruit, and nuts, if desired, into the batter by hand just until combined.

Scrape the batter into the prepared pan. Bake for 50 to 60 minutes or until a toothpick inserted in the center of the loaf comes out clean. The crust may crack. Cool the bread in the pan set on a wire rack for about 10 minutes. Turn out onto a wire rack and cool completely.

For a morning dose of vitamin C and fiber, we wake up to freshly baked loaves of this oatmeal bread lightly kissed with orange. The point-counterpoint of the sweet bananas and the zingy orange flavor makes it a delicious eye-opener. Now if we could only decide who gets up first to bake!

1 cup plus 1 tablespoon old-fashioned rolled oats

¾ cup orange juice

2 cups unbleached all-purpose flour

1 teaspoon baking powder

1 teaspoon baking soda

¼ teaspoon salt

1 large egg

2 large egg whites

½ cup packed brown sugar

¼ cup honey

2 tablespoons vegetable oil

1 teaspoon grated orange rind

1 cup mashed ripe bananas (about 2 large bananas)

½ cup golden raisins

Stir 1 cup oats into the orange juice and set aside.

Preheat the oven to 350°F. Coat a 9-by-5-inch loaf pan with nonstick cooking spray.

Whisk the flour with the baking powder, baking soda, and salt and set aside.

Beat the egg, egg whites, brown sugar, honey, and oil with an electric mixer set at medium until smooth. Add the orange rind and bananas and beat again. Stir the flour, oats, and raisins into the batter by hand just until combined.

Scrape the batter into the prepared pan. Sprinkle it with the remaining 1 tablespoon oats. Bake for 50 to 60 minutes or until a toothpick inserted in the center of the loaf comes out clean. The crust may crack. Cool the bread in the pan set on a wire rack for about 10 minutes. Turn out onto a wire rack and cool completely.

# Good Morning Sunshine Bread

**Yield:** 1 loaf; 14 slices

**Calories per slice:** 181

**Fat per slice:** 3 grams

**Percent of calories from fat:** 15%

# Banana–Oat Bran Bread

**Yield:** 1 loaf; 14 slices

**Calories per slice:** 159

**Fat per slice:** 3 grams

**Percent of calories from fat:** 17%

Considering their global popularity, it's a lucky thing bananas are so healthful. The potassium alone makes them well worth eating, as the mineral helps nourish muscles and is particularly beneficial to the heart. Bananas also contain the stress-reducing essential amino acid tryptophan. When teamed with fiber-filled oats and oat bran, they bake into a super good-for-you-bread that (need we say?) tastes great.

1⅔ cups unbleached all-purpose flour

⅔ cup plus 1 tablespoon old-fashioned rolled oats

⅔ cup oat bran

1½ teaspoons baking soda

1 teaspoon ground cinnamon

½ teaspoon grated nutmeg

¼ teaspoon salt

1 large egg

1 large egg white

⅔ cup packed brown sugar

2 tablespoons vegetable oil

½ cup buttermilk

1¼ cups mashed ripe bananas (about 3 bananas)

Preheat the oven to 350°F. Coat a 9-by-5-inch loaf pan with nonstick cooking spray.

Whisk the flour with ⅔ cup oats, the oat bran, baking soda, cinnamon, nutmeg, and salt and set aside.

Beat the egg, egg white, brown sugar, and oil with an electric mixer set at medium until smooth. Add the buttermilk and bananas and beat again. Stir the flour mixture into the batter by hand just until combined.

Scrape the batter into the prepared pan. Sprinkle it with the remaining 1 tablespoon oats. Bake for 50 to 60 minutes or until a toothpick inserted in the center of the loaf comes out clean. The crust may crack. Cool the bread in the pan set on a wire rack for about 10 minutes. Turn out onto a wire rack and cool completely.

If you read the introductory note to Banana-Oat Bran Bread, you know how important we think bananas are. Now we'll tell you how important chocolate is! (Very, very, very.) Many thanks to Rose Thal for sharing this moist, sweet, delicious, incredible bread with us. It's one of our favorite ways to get our daily minimum requirement of bananas and chocolate.

2 cups unbleached all-purpose flour
1½ teaspoons baking powder
1 teaspoon baking soda
¼ teaspoon salt
1 large egg
2 large egg whites
1⅓ cups sugar
2 tablespoons vegetable oil
⅓ cup nonfat gelatin-free plain yogurt
1¼ cups mashed ripe bananas (about 3 bananas)
¾ cup semisweet chocolate chips

Preheat the oven to 350°F. Coat a 9-by-5-inch loaf pan with nonstick cooking spray.

Whisk the flour with the baking powder, baking soda, and salt and set aside.

Beat the egg, egg whites, sugar, and oil with an electric mixer set at medium until smooth. Add the yogurt and bananas and beat again. Stir the flour and chocolate chips into the batter by hand just until combined.

Scrape the batter into the prepared pan. Bake for about 1 hour and 15 to 20 minutes or until a toothpick inserted in the center of the loaf comes out clean. The crust may crack. Cool the bread in the pan set on a wire rack for about 10 minutes. Turn out onto a wire rack and cool completely.

# Chocolate Chip—Banana Bread

Yield: 1 loaf; 14 slices

Calories per slice: 220

Fat per slice: 5.3 grams

Percent of calories from fat: 22%

# Dr. Cookie's Plum Crazy Bread

Yield: 1 loaf; 14 slices

Calories per slice: 146

Fat per slice: 1 gram

Percent of calories from fat: 6%

You would be "plum crazy" if you didn't go wild for this fruity bread. Use the small purple plums sometimes called prune plums or Italian plums rather than larger red- or yellow-skinned plums. The purple ones separate more easily from their pits and hold up during baking. You can also substitute nectarines or peaches for the plums.

2 cups unbleached all-purpose flour

1 tablespoon baking powder

½ teaspoon baking soda

½ teaspoon ground cinnamon

1 cup quick-cooking oats

½ teaspoon salt

1 cup diced plums (about 5 to 6 plums)

1 large egg

2 large egg whites

¾ cup packed brown sugar

1½ cups nonfat gelatin-free plain yogurt

Preheat the oven to 350°F. Coat a 9-by-5-inch loaf pan with nonstick cooking spray.

Whisk the flour with the baking powder, baking soda, cinnamon, oats, and salt. Add the plums and toss gently to coat. Set aside.

Beat the egg, egg whites, brown sugar, and yogurt with an electric mixer set at medium until smooth. Stir the flour and plums into the batter by hand just until combined.

Scrape the batter into the prepared pan. Bake for 50 to 60 minutes or until a toothpick inserted in the center of the loaf comes out clean. The crust may crack. Cool the bread in the pan set on a wire rack for about 10 minutes. Turn out onto a wire rack and cool completely.

**N**o doubt about it. *Prunes are good for you. They are an excellent source of dietary fiber and provide substantial amounts of beta-carotene (vitamin A) and potassium. They are so naturally sweet, less sugar is required in recipes using them. Prune puree can be used in place of oil in many recipes—including this tasty one.*

¼ cup pitted whole prunes

¼ cup very hot (not boiling) water

1 cup old-fashioned rolled oats

1¼ cups buttermilk

2 cups unbleached all-purpose flour

1 tablespoon baking powder

1 teaspoon baking soda

¼ teaspoon salt

½ cup chopped pitted prunes

1 large egg

1 large egg white

½ cup packed brown sugar

1 teaspoon vanilla extract

Preheat the oven to 350°F. Coat a 9-by-5-inch loaf pan with nonstick cooking spray.

Soak the whole prunes in the hot water for about 10 minutes. Puree the prunes and any hot water not absorbed by them in a blender until smooth.

Stir the oats into the buttermilk and let sit for 5 minutes.

Whisk the flour with the baking powder, baking soda, and salt. Add the chopped prunes and toss gently to coat. Set aside.

Beat the egg, egg white, and brown sugar with an electric mixer set at medium until smooth. Add the prune puree, oats-buttermilk mixture, and vanilla and beat again. Stir the flour and prunes into the batter by hand just until combined.

Scrape the batter into the prepared pan. Bake for 50 to 60 minutes or until a toothpick inserted in the center of the loaf comes out clean. The crust may crack. Cool the bread in the pan set on a wire rack for about 10 minutes. Turn out onto a wire rack and cool completely.

# Prune Bread

<u>Yield:</u> 1 loaf; 14 slices

<u>Calories per slice:</u> 150

<u>Fat per slice:</u> 1.1 grams

<u>Percent of calories from fat:</u> 7%

159

Quick Breads

# Date-No-Nut Bread

**Yield:** 1 loaf; 14 slices

**Calories per slice:** 167

**Fat per slice:** 3.4 grams

**Percent of calories from fat:** 18%

*We left the nuts out of date-nut bread to save calories and fat—but at no sacrifice to flavor. A cup of nuts has about 760 calories and 72 grams of fat. Whew! If you crave date-nut bread with nuts, add about ¼ cup of chopped nuts to the batter when you stir in the flour. Include the extra calories and fat when you figure your daily or weekly calorie and fat intake.*

1½ cups unbleached all-purpose flour

½ cup whole wheat flour

1 cup wheat germ

1 tablespoon baking powder

1 teaspoon baking soda

½ teaspoon salt

¾ cup chopped dates

2 large egg whites

⅓ cup honey

2 tablespoons vegetable oil

1 cup buttermilk

Preheat the oven to 350°F. Coat a 9-by-5-inch loaf pan with nonstick cooking spray.

Whisk the flours with the wheat germ, baking powder, baking soda, and salt. Add the dates and toss gently to coat. Set aside.

Beat the egg whites, honey, and oil with an electric mixer set at medium until smooth. Add the buttermilk and beat again. Stir the flour and dates into the batter by hand just until combined.

Scrape the batter into the prepared pan. Bake for 40 to 50 minutes or until a toothpick inserted in the center of the loaf comes out clean. The crust may crack. Cool the bread in the pan set on a wire rack for about 10 minutes. Turn out onto a wire rack and cool completely.

This is a lighter date bread than the preceding recipe and has slightly more dates. It's also jazzed up with our favorite spices. This is one "date" that turns into a dream come true.

2½ cups unbleached all-purpose flour
1 tablespoon baking powder
½ teaspoon baking soda
2 teaspoons ground cinnamon
½ teaspoon grated nutmeg
¼ teaspoon salt
1 cup chopped dates
1 large egg
1 large egg white
⅔ cup packed brown sugar
2 tablespoons vegetable oil
1 cup buttermilk

Preheat the oven to 325°F. Coat a 9-by-5-inch loaf pan with nonstick cooking spray.

Whisk the flour with the baking powder, baking soda, cinnamon, nutmeg, and salt. Add the dates and toss gently to coat. Set aside.

Beat the egg, egg white, brown sugar, and oil with an electric mixer set at medium until smooth. Add the buttermilk and beat again. Stir the flour and dates into the batter by hand just until combined.

Scrape the batter into the prepared pan. Bake for 45 to 50 minutes or until a toothpick inserted in the center of the loaf comes out clean. The crust may crack. Cool the bread in the pan set on a wire rack for about 10 minutes. Turn out onto a wire rack and cool completely.

# "Blind Date" Bread

<u>Yield:</u> 1 loaf; 14 slices

<u>Calories per slice:</u> 179

<u>Fat per slice:</u> 2.9 grams

<u>Percent of calories from fat:</u> 15%

# Carrot-Oatmeal Bread

Yield: I loaf; 14 slices

Calories per slice: 157

Fat per slice: 3 grams

Percent of calories from fat: 17%

*Don't be put off from trying this excellent recipe because of the long list of ingredients. Everything on it is easy to find and the baked bread is loaded with dietary fiber and beta-carotene (vitamin A).*

1 cup plus 1 tablespoon old-fashioned rolled oats

1 cup buttermilk

2 cups unbleached all-purpose flour

1 tablespoon baking powder

1 teaspoon baking soda

1 teaspoon ground cinnamon

½ teaspoon grated nutmeg

¼ teaspoon salt

1 large egg

2 large egg whites

⅓ cup packed brown sugar

⅓ cup honey

2 tablespoons vegetable oil

1 teaspoon vanilla extract

1½ cups grated unpeeled carrots (about 3 to 4 carrots)

Preheat the oven to 350°F. Coat a 9-by-5-inch loaf pan with nonstick cooking spray.

Stir the oats into the buttermilk and let sit for 5 minutes.

Whisk the flour with the baking powder, baking soda, cinnamon, nutmeg, and salt and set aside.

Beat the egg, egg whites, brown sugar, honey, and oil with an electric mixer set at medium until smooth. Add the oat-buttermilk mixture, vanilla, and carrots and beat again. Stir the flour into the batter by hand just until combined.

Scrape the batter into the prepared pan. Sprinkle it with the remaining 1 tablespoon oats. Bake for 50 to 55 minutes or until a toothpick inserted in the center of the loaf comes out clean. The crust may crack. Cool the bread in the pan set on a wire rack for about 10 minutes. Turn out onto a wire rack and cool completely.

G̲et the day off to a winning start with this high-rising loaf of moist carrot bread. The citrus rind offsets the carrot's sweetness and the zucchini adds a lovely mellowness. Our families love it toasted.

2½ cups unbleached all-purpose flour
1 cup whole wheat flour
1 tablespoon baking powder
1 teaspoon baking soda
¼ teaspoon salt
1 large egg
2 large egg whites
½ cup packed brown sugar
2 tablespoons vegetable oil
1½ cups buttermilk
1 teaspoon grated lemon rind
1 teaspoon grated orange rind
1 cup shredded carrot (about 2 carrots)
1 cup shredded zucchini (about 1 to 2 medium zucchini)
¼ cup chopped walnuts (optional)

Preheat the oven to 350°F. Coat a 9-by-5-inch loaf pan with nonstick cooking spray.

Whisk the flours with the baking powder, baking soda, and salt and set aside.

Beat the egg, egg whites, brown sugar, and oil with an electric mixer set at medium until smooth. Add the buttermilk, lemon rind, and orange rind and beat again. Stir the flour, carrot, zucchini, and nuts, if desired, into the batter by hand just until combined.

Scrape the batter into the prepared pan. Bake for 55 to 60 minutes or until a toothpick inserted in the center of the loaf comes out clean. The crust may crack. Cool the bread in the pan set on a wire rack for about 10 minutes. Turn out onto a wire rack and cool completely.

# Carrot-Zucchini Bread

Yield: 1 loaf; 14 slices

Calories per slice:
171 without walnuts; 185 with walnuts

Fat per slice:
3 grams without walnuts; 4.4 grams with walnuts

Percent of calories from fat:
16% without walnuts; 21% with walnuts

# Corn Bread in the Round

Yield: 1 round loaf; 8 wedges

Calories per wedge: 168

Fat per wedge: 4.3 grams

Percent of calories from fat: 23%

Nothing beats corn bread right from the oven. But this round loaf is almost as good toasted the next day. For variety, add a half-cup of chopped red or green bell peppers to the batter with the dry ingredients. A half-cup of cranberries is another good idea and makes this ideal for Thanksgiving. It looks pretty, too!

1 cup yellow cornmeal

1 cup unbleached all-purpose flour

5 teaspoons baking powder

¼ teaspoon salt

1 large egg

¼ cup honey

2 tablespoons vegetable oil

1 cup skim milk

Preheat the oven to 350°F. Coat a 9-inch pie pan with nonstick cooking spray.

Whisk the cornmeal with the flour, baking powder, and salt and set aside.

Beat the egg, honey, and oil with an electric mixer set at medium until smooth. Add the milk and beat again. Stir the cornmeal mixture into the batter by hand just until combined. The batter will be lumpy.

Scrape the batter into the prepared pan. Bake for 20 to 30 minutes or until lightly browned and a toothpick inserted in the center of the loaf comes out clean. Cut the hot bread into wedges and serve right away.

*The chives and the carrots make this corn bread something special. Try it with robust vegetable soups or chili.*

1 cup yellow cornmeal

1½ cups unbleached all-purpose flour

1 tablespoon baking powder

1½ teaspoons baking soda

2 teaspoons marjoram leaves

2 teaspoons chopped chives, or 2 tablespoons chopped green onion

¼ teaspoon salt

1 large egg

1 large egg white

2 tablespoons packed brown sugar

2 tablespoons vegetable oil

1 cup buttermilk

1 cup shredded carrot (about 1 carrot)

Preheat the oven to 350°F. Coat a 9-by-5-inch loaf pan with nonstick cooking spray.

Whisk the cornmeal with the flour, baking powder, baking soda, marjoram, chives or green onion, and salt and set aside.

Beat the egg, egg white, brown sugar, and oil with an electric mixer set at medium until smooth. Add the buttermilk and carrots and beat again. Stir the cornmeal mixture into the batter by hand just until combined.

Scrape the batter into the prepared pan. Bake for 45 to 50 minutes or until lightly browned and a toothpick inserted in the center of the loaf comes out clean. The crust may crack. Cool the bread in the pan set on a wire rack for about 10 minutes. Turn out onto a wire rack and cool completely.

# Spicy Corn Bread

<u>Yield:</u> 1 loaf; 14 slices

<u>Calories per slice:</u> 121

<u>Fat per slice:</u> 2.5 grams

<u>Percent of calories from fat:</u> 19%

# Hiking Bread

**Yield:** 1 loaf; 14 slices

**Calories per slice:** 153

**Fat per slice:** .5 gram

**Percent of calories from fat:** 3%

*We highly recommend this bread for a quick energy snack when you are hiking, biking, or taking a rambling walk through the park. It's nice and firm so it will not crumble when packed in a knapsack or brown bag. And it tastes wonderful spread with low-fat cream cheese or eaten plain. The rye flour gives it a robustness not always found in quick breads.*

1 cup unbleached all-purpose flour

1 cup rye flour

1¼ teaspoons baking powder

1 teaspoon baking soda

¼ teaspoon salt

1½ cups nonfat gelatin-free plain yogurt

2 tablespoons packed brown sugar

¼ cup light molasses

1½ cups old-fashioned rolled oats

1 cup raisins

Preheat the oven to 350°F. Coat a 9-by-5-inch loaf pan with nonstick cooking spray.

Whisk the flours with the baking powder, baking soda, and salt and set aside.

Beat the yogurt, brown sugar, and molasses with an electric mixer set at medium until smooth. Add the oats and beat again. Stir the flour and raisins into the batter by hand just until combined.

Scrape the batter into the prepared pan and let it sit for 20 minutes. Bake for 45 to 55 minutes or until lightly browned and the bread pulls away from the sides of the pan. Turn out onto a wire rack and cool completely.

Pumpkins and apricots are both good sources of beta-carotene (vitamin A). They also are high in fiber. Wheat germ is the center of the wheat berry—the part that is left after the hull, bran, and endosperm are stripped away. Of all parts of the grain, the germ contains the most essential oils, minerals, and vitamins. What do all these facts mean? The bread is good for you! And it's a treat to eat, too.

1⅓ cups unbleached all-purpose flour

⅔ cup plus 1 tablespoon old-fashioned rolled oats

¼ cup wheat germ

1 teaspoon baking powder

1 teaspoon baking soda

½ teaspoon ground allspice

½ teaspoon grated nutmeg

½ teaspoon ground cinnamon

¼ teaspoon salt

1 large egg

1 large egg white

½ cup packed brown sugar

¼ cup granulated sugar

2 tablespoons vegetable oil

⅓ cup skim milk

1¼ cups unsweetened pumpkin puree

½ cup chopped dried apricots

¼ cup chopped pecans (optional)

Preheat the oven to 350°F. Coat a 9-by-5-inch loaf pan with nonstick cooking spray.

Whisk the flour with ⅔ cup of the oats, the wheat germ, baking powder, baking soda, allspice, nutmeg, cinnamon, and salt and set aside.

Beat the egg, egg white, sugars, and oil with an electric mixer set at medium until smooth. Add the milk and pumpkin and beat again. Stir the flour, apricots, and pecans, if desired, into the batter by hand just until combined.

Scrape the batter into the prepared pan. Sprinkle it with the remaining 1 tablespoon oats. Bake for 45 to 50 minutes or until a toothpick inserted

(continued)

# Pumpkin-Oat Bread

Yield: 1 loaf; 14 slices

Calories per slice:
153 without pecans; 167 with pecans

Fat per slice:
2.8 grams without pecans; 3.5 grams with pecans

Percent of calories from fat:
16% without pecans; 19% with pecans

in the center of the loaf comes out clean. The crust may crack. Cool the bread in the pan set on a wire rack for about 10 minutes. Turn out onto a wire rack and cool completely.

# Wild Rice Bread

**Yield:** 1 loaf; 14 slices
**Calories per slice:** 146
**Fat per slice:** 1 gram
**Percent of calories from fat:** 6%

*Wild rice adds earthy, nutty flavor and a little crunch to this prune-sweetened bread.*

¼ cup pitted prunes
¼ cup very hot (not boiling) water
2 cups unbleached all-purpose flour
1 tablespoon baking powder
½ teaspoon baking soda
½ teaspoon salt
1 large egg
1 large egg white
⅔ cup packed brown sugar
1¼ cups buttermilk
1 teaspoon vanilla extract
1 cup cooked and cooled wild rice

Soak the prunes in the hot water for about 10 minutes. Puree the prunes and any hot water not absorbed by them in a blender until smooth.

Preheat the oven to 350°F. Coat a 9-by-5-inch loaf pan with nonstick cooking spray.

Whisk the flour with baking powder, baking soda, and salt and set aside.

Beat the egg, egg white, and brown sugar with an electric mixer set at medium until smooth. Add the buttermilk, vanilla, and prune puree and beat again. Stir the flour and wild rice into the batter by hand just until combined.

Scrape the batter into the prepared pan. Bake for 50 to 60 minutes or until a toothpick inserted in the center of the loaf comes out clean. The crust may crack. Cool the bread in the pan set on a wire rack for about 10 minutes. Turn out onto a wire rack and cool completely.

*R*ich orange vegetables such as yams and sweet potatoes are great for beta-carotene (vitamin A) and vitamin E. They also make deliciously moist breads. See if your friends can guess what the "secret" ingredient (yams) is in this delightful loaf.

1¼ cups unbleached all-purpose flour

1 cup whole wheat flour

1½ teaspoons baking powder

1 teaspoon baking soda

¼ teaspoon salt

1 large egg

2 large egg whites

1 cup packed brown sugar

2 tablespoons vegetable oil

1 teaspoon vanilla extract

1 generous cup mashed cooked yam (an 8- to 9-ounce yam)

½ cup golden raisins

Preheat the oven to 350°F. Coat a 9-by-5-inch loaf pan with nonstick cooking spray.

Whisk the flours with baking powder, baking soda, and salt and set aside.

Beat the egg, egg whites, brown sugar, and oil with an electric mixer set at medium until smooth. Add the vanilla and mashed yam and beat again. Stir the flour and raisins into the batter by hand just until combined.

Scrape the batter into the prepared pan. Bake for 40 to 50 minutes or until a toothpick inserted in the center of the loaf comes out clean. The crust may crack. Cool the bread in the pan set on a wire rack for about 10 minutes. Turn out onto a wire rack and cool completely.

# Yummy Yam Bread

<u>Yield:</u> 1 loaf; 14 slices

<u>Calories per slice:</u> 174

<u>Fat per slice:</u> 2.5 grams

<u>Percent of calories from fat:</u> 13%

# Zucchini Bread

**Yield:** 1 loaf; 14 slices

**Calories per slice:** 138

**Fat per slice:** 3.8 grams

**Percent of calories from fat:** 25%

Zucchini bread is almost an American classic and we could not put together a cookbook without a recipe. But the difference between ours and other recipes is that this one is low in fat—but not in taste.

1½ cups unbleached all-purpose flour

2 teaspoons baking powder

½ teaspoon baking soda

¼ teaspoon grated nutmeg

¼ teaspoon ground ginger

1 large egg

½ cup honey

2 tablespoons vegetable oil

½ cup nonfat gelatin-free plain yogurt

1 teaspoon grated lemon rind

1 teaspoon grated orange rind

1 cup shredded zucchini (1 to 2 medium zucchini)

½ cup raisins

¼ cup chopped walnuts

Preheat the oven to 350°F. Coat a 9-by-5-inch loaf pan with nonstick cooking spray.

Whisk the flour with baking powder, baking soda, nutmeg, and ginger and set aside.

Beat the egg, honey, and oil with an electric mixer set at medium until smooth. Add the yogurt, lemon rind, and orange rind and beat again. Stir the flour, zucchini, raisins, and walnuts into the batter by hand just until combined.

Scrape the batter into the prepared pan. Bake for 40 to 45 minutes or until a toothpick inserted in the center of the loaf comes out clean. The crust may crack. Cool the bread in the pan set on a wire rack for about 10 minutes. Turn out onto a wire rack and cool completely.

We are constantly coming up with ways to bake with zucchini, since the tenacious squash has the propensity to overtake our gardens every year. With the addition of tangy pineapple and judicious amounts of spices, this is a bread to be reckoned with.

½ cup unsweetened crushed pineapple, drained

½ cup raisins

1½ cups unbleached all-purpose flour

1 teaspoon baking powder

½ teaspoon baking soda

1 teaspoon ground cinnamon

½ teaspoon grated nutmeg

¼ teaspoon ground ginger

¼ teaspoon salt

1 large egg

1 large egg white

⅓ cup packed brown sugar

2 tablespoons vegetable oil

¼ cup honey

1 teaspoon vanilla extract

1 cup shredded zucchini (1 to 2 medium zucchini)

Preheat the oven to 350°F. Coat a 9-by-5-inch loaf pan with nonstick cooking spray.

Toss the pineapple with the raisins and set aside.

Whisk the flour with the baking powder, baking soda, cinnamon, nutmeg, ginger, and salt and set aside.

Beat the egg, egg white, brown sugar, and oil with an electric mixer set at medium until smooth. Add the honey and vanilla and beat again. Drain any accumulated juice from the pineapple-raisin mixture. Stir the flour, pineapple-raisin mixture, and zucchini into the batter by hand just until combined.

Scrape the batter into the prepared pan. Bake for 45 to 55 minutes or until a toothpick inserted in the center of the loaf comes out clean. The crust may crack. Cool the bread in the pan set on a wire rack for about 10 minutes. Turn out onto a wire rack and cool completely.

# Zucchini-Pineapple Bread

<u>Yield:</u> 1 loaf; 14 slices

<u>Calories per slice:</u> 146

<u>Fat per slice:</u> 2.9 grams

<u>Percent of calories from fat:</u> 18%

# Zucchini-Oat-Banana Bread

Yield: 1 loaf; 14 slices

Calories per slice:
    177 with walnuts; 177 with oat topping

Fat per slice:
    3.8 grams with walnuts; 2.6 grams with oat topping

Percent of calories from fat:
    19% with walnuts; 13% with oat topping

*For this bread, as for all breads with bananas, the riper the fruit, the sweeter the flavor. Using milk-soaked oats on the bread results in a nice, crunchy topping that is much lower in fat than traditional streusel toppings.*

2 cups unbleached all-purpose flour
1 cup old-fashioned rolled oats
2 teaspoons baking powder
½ teaspoon baking soda
1 teaspoon ground cinnamon
¼ teaspoon salt
2 large egg whites
¾ cup packed brown sugar
2 tablespoons vegetable oil
1 cup nonfat gelatin-free plain yogurt
1 cup mashed ripe bananas (about 2 bananas)
¾ cup shredded zucchini (1 to 1½ medium zucchini)
¼ cup chopped walnuts, or ½ cup old-fashioned rolled oats soaked in ¼ cup skim milk

Preheat the oven to 350°F. Coat a 9-by-5-inch loaf pan with nonstick cooking spray.

Whisk the flour with the oats, baking powder, baking soda, cinnamon, and salt and set aside.

Beat the egg whites, brown sugar, and oil with an electric mixer set at medium until smooth. Add the yogurt and bananas, and beat again. Stir the flour and zucchini into the batter by hand just until combined.

Scrape the batter into the prepared pan. Top with the walnuts or soaked oats. Bake for 50 to 55 minutes or until a toothpick inserted in the center of the loaf comes out clean. The crust may crack. Cool the bread in the pan set on a wire rack for about 10 minutes. Turn out onto a wire rack and cool completely.

When we first tasted maple-flavored zucchini bread, we fell in love. But when we analyzed the recipe, we discovered this was a doomed affair. There were 263 calories in every slice and 14 grams of fat! After some trial and error we came up with a recipe that reduces the calories to 183 per slice and the fat to a mere 4 grams. And guess what? It's every bit as seductively delicious! Ain't love grand?

1½ cups unbleached all-purpose flour
½ cup whole wheat flour
¼ cup wheat germ
1 teaspoon baking powder
1 teaspoon baking soda
¼ teaspoon salt
¼ cup chopped walnuts (optional)
½ cup raisins
1 tablespoon plus 1 teaspoon sesame seeds
1 large egg
1 large egg white
½ cup packed brown sugar
½ cup granulated sugar
2 tablespoons vegetable oil
¾ cup buttermilk
1 tablespoon maple extract
1½ cups shredded zucchini (1 to 2 medium zucchini)

Preheat the oven to 350°F. Coat a 9-by-5-inch loaf pan with nonstick cooking spray.

Whisk the flours with the wheat germ, baking powder, baking soda, and salt. Add the walnuts, if desired, raisins, and 1 tablespoon sesame seeds and toss gently. Set aside.

Beat the egg, egg white, sugars, and oil with an electric mixer set at medium until smooth. Add the buttermilk and maple extract and beat again. Stir the flour mixture and zucchini into the batter by hand just until combined.

(continued)

# Zucchini-Maple Bread

Yield: 1 loaf; 14 slices

Calories per slice:
170 without walnuts; 183 with walnuts

Fat per slice:
2.8 grams without walnuts; 4 grams with walnuts

Percent of calories from fat:
15% without walnuts; 20% with walnuts

Scrape the batter into the prepared pan. Top with the remaining teaspoon of sesame seeds. Bake for 50 to 55 minutes or until a toothpick inserted in the center of the loaf comes out clean. The crust may crack. Cool the bread in the pan set on a wire rack for about 10 minutes. Turn out onto a wire rack and cool completely.

# Chapter 7

# Yeast Breads

**W**hat smells better than baking bread? Hardly anything. Okay, we admit that the smell of baking cookies comes first in our affections, but bread runs a close second. Its warm, yeasty aroma fills the house, making everyone feel safe and nurtured.

We have always liked to make bread. Kneading the pliant dough into a smooth mass is earthy, satisfying, and so "real." We scoffed at bread machines: who needed them? But one day curiosity overcame prejudice and we tried one. What a discovery! The machine does all the hard work, saving time and energy and making it possible to have fresh bread every day. We dislike the funny-shaped loaves that come out of the bread machine and so usually remove the perfectly kneaded dough from it, shape it, and let it rise for the second time in a bread pan before baking it in the conventional oven. Sometimes we get real lazy and let the machine complete its cycle. The bread still tastes good! We don't recommend leaving the machine on when you're not in the house. It requires some watching, as we found one day when we arrived home just in time to stop an out-of-control recipe from rising over the lip of the inner pan.

Our recipes for yeast breads begin with traditional instructions for making bread by hand. For almost every recipe we also have instructions for making the same loaf in the bread machine. Use our proportions, but follow your machine's particular directions for the order in which the ingredients should be put in the bread pan: some begin with yeast, others end with yeast.

Not surprisingly, our breads include lots of whole grains, bran, rice, oats, and other nutrient-packed and fiber-rich products. We also have an enticing variety of vegetable and fruit breads. Some are great for sandwiches, others are better for toasting, and still others make scrumptious dinner rolls.

This is our favorite basic bread recipe that we change depending on our appetites. Add a half-cup more or less whole wheat flour for a fuller flavored or milder loaf. Substitute molasses, brown sugar, or maple syrup for the honey. Experiment and have fun with this bread. It's always delicious.

- 2 cups unbleached all-purpose flour
- 1½ cups whole wheat flour
- 1 teaspoon salt
- 2 tablespoons vegetable oil
- ¼ cup honey
- 1 ¼-ounce package active dry yeast (1 scant tablespoon), at room temperature
- 1¼ cups warm water

Mix all the ingredients except 1 cup of all-purpose flour in a large bowl. Stir with a large spoon or spatula and when the dough is cohesive, turn it out onto a lightly floured surface.

Knead the dough for 10 to 15 minutes or until it is smooth and elastic. Add as much of the reserved flour as necessary to keep the dough from sticking.

Put the dough into a large, lightly oiled bowl, cover with a kitchen towel, and let rise in a warm, draft-free place for about 1 hour or until doubled in volume.

*Coat a 9-by-5-inch loaf pan with nonstick cooking spray.

Using your fist, gently punch down the risen dough. Turn the dough out onto a lightly floured surface and knead for about 1 minute. Shape the dough into a loaf and put in the pan. Cover and let rise in a warm, draft-free place for 45 to 60 minutes or until again doubled in volume.

Alternatively, shape the dough into a freestanding, round loaf and place on a baking sheet that has been coated with nonstick cooking spray. Or divide the dough into 3 sections for braiding. To braid, stretch and roll each section into a strand. Lay the strands on a lightly floured surface so that they are attatched at one end. Braid them and fold under the ends. Carefully lift the braid and set it on a baking sheet that has been coated with nonstick cooking spray. Or divide the dough into 10 pieces and roll each one into a roll. Set the rolls about 1 inch apart on a baking sheet that

(continued)

# Whole Wheat Bread

**Yield:** 1 loaf; 18 slices

**Calories per slice:** 140

**Fat per slice:** 1.9 grams

**Percent of calories from fat:** 16%

177

Yeast Breads

has been coated with nonstick cooking spray. Cover the free-form loaf, braid, or rolls and let rise in a warm, draft-free place for 45 to 60 minutes or until almost doubled in volume.

Preheat the oven to 350°F.

Bake the rectangular or free-form loaf for 40 to 45 minutes, the braid for 30 to 40 minutes, and rolls for 20 to 30 minutes; or until the bread is lightly browned and sounds hollow when tapped. Remove the bread from the pan and let cool on a wire rack.

~·~

**To Make in a Bread Machine:** Put all the ingredients in the bread pan in the order listed. (If your machine's manual instructs you to add the ingredients in the reverse order, follow the manual.) Select the basic bread setting and push the start button.

If you prefer to bake the bread in the oven or shape it and bake in the oven, select the dough (or manual) setting. Remove the dough from the machine after it rises once. Follow the instructions beginning at the asterisk (*).

# Honey-Oat Bread

**Yield:** 1 loaf; 18 slices

**Calories per slice:**
103 without almonds; 113 with almonds

**Fat per slice:**
1.3 grams without almonds; 2 grams with almonds

**Percent of calories from fat:**
11% without almonds; 16% with almonds

**A**s you no doubt realize by now, oats are a Dr. Cookie high-fiber favorite. Plus they make baked goods taste good. The almonds provide optional, extra crunch.

1 ¼-ounce package active dry yeast (1 scant tablespoon)

1¼ cups warm water

¼ cup honey

1 cup old-fashioned rolled oats

2 cups unbleached all-purpose flour

1 cup whole wheat flour

1 tablespoon vegetable oil

1 teaspoon salt

¼ cup chopped almonds (optional)

Dissolve the yeast in ½ cup warm water. Stir in 1 tablespoon honey. Set aside for about 5 minutes or until bubbly.

Mix the remaining ingredients except 1 cup of all-purpose flour in a large bowl. Add the yeast mixture. Stir with a large spoon or spatula and when the dough is cohesive, turn it out onto a lightly floured surface.

Knead the dough for 10 to 15 minutes or until it is smooth and elastic. Add as much of the reserved flour as necessary to keep the dough from sticking.

Put the dough in a large, lightly oiled bowl, cover with a kitchen towel, and let rise in a warm, draft-free place for about 1 hour or until doubled in volume.

*Coat a 9-by-5-inch loaf pan with nonstick cooking spray.

Using your fist, gently punch down the risen dough. Turn the dough out onto a lightly floured surface and knead for about 1 minute. Shape the dough into a loaf and put in the pan. Cover and let rise in a warm, draft-free place for 45 to 60 minutes or until again doubled in volume.

Preheat the oven to 350°F.

Bake the loaf for about 40 minutes or until the bread is lightly browned and sounds hollow when tapped. Remove the bread from the pan and let cool on a wire rack.

~·~

**To Make in a Bread Machine:** Put all the ingredients in the bread pan in the order listed. (If your machine's manual instructs you to add the ingredients in the reverse order, follow the manual.) Select the basic bread setting and push the start button.

If you prefer to bake the bread in the oven or shape it and bake in the oven, select the dough (or manual) setting. Remove the dough from the machine after it rises once. Follow the instructions beginning at the asterisk (*).

# Wheat Germ—Herb Bread

Yield: 1 loaf; 18 slices

Calories per slice: 99

Fat per slice: 2.2 grams

Percent of calories from fat: 20%

**B**ecause wheat germ contains the essential oils contained in the wheat berry, it turns rancid more quickly than any other part of the wheat. It's important to store wheat germ in the refrigerator or, for longer storage, the freezer. It keeps in the refrigerator for about a month and two or three times that in the freezer. Let it come to room temperature before using in the recipe.

2 cups unbleached all-purpose flour

1 cup whole wheat flour

½ cup plus 2 tablespoons wheat germ, at room temperature

2 tablespoons packed brown sugar

2 tablespoons vegetable oil

1 teaspoon salt

½ teaspoon dried thyme

½ teaspoon dried marjoram

1 ¼-ounce package active dry yeast (1 scant tablespoon), at room temperature

1 ¼ cups warm water

1 large egg white, lightly beaten

Mix 1 cup all-purpose flour, the whole wheat flour, ½ cup wheat germ, the brown sugar, oil, salt, thyme, marjoram, yeast, and warm water in a large bowl. Stir with a large spoon or spatula and when the dough is cohesive, turn it out onto a lightly floured surface.

Knead the dough for 10 to 15 minutes or until it is smooth and elastic. Add as much of the reserved cup of flour as necessary to keep the dough from sticking.

Put the dough in a large, lightly oiled bowl, cover with a kitchen towel, and let rise in a warm, draft-free place for about 1 hour or until doubled in volume.

*Coat a 9-by-5-inch loaf pan with nonstick cooking spray.

Using your fist, gently punch down the risen dough. Turn the dough out onto a lightly floured surface and knead for about 1 minute. Shape the dough into a loaf and put in the pan. Cover and let rise in a warm, draft-free place for 45 to 60 minutes or until again doubled in volume.

Preheat the oven to 350°F.

Brush the top of the loaf with the egg white and sprinkle with the remaining 2 tablespoons wheat germ. Bake the loaf for about 40 minutes or until the bread is lightly browned and sounds hollow when tapped. Remove the bread from the pan and let cool on a wire rack.

~~

**To Make in a Bread Machine:** Put all the ingredients, except the egg white and 2 tablespoons wheat germ, in the bread pan in the order listed. (If your machine's manual instructs you to add the ingredients in the reverse order, follow the manual.) Select the basic bread setting and push the start button.

If you prefer to bake the bread in the oven or shape it and bake in the oven, select the dough (or manual) setting. Remove the dough from the machine after it rises once. Follow the instructions beginning at the asterisk (*).

# Herbed Flat-bread

Yield: 1 loaf; 18 slices

Calories per slice: 63

Fat per slice: 1 gram

Percent of calories from fat: 14%

We love this low-fat bread as an appetizer loaf. Try it with roasted red peppers and marinated mushrooms, or a little low-fat cheese. It's splendid by itself, too.

1 ¼-ounce package active dry yeast (1 scant tablespoon), at room temperature

1 cup warm water

1 teaspoon sugar

1¾ cups unbleached all-purpose flour

½ cup whole wheat flour

1½ teaspoons dried basil

1 teaspoon salt

1 tablespoon olive oil

Freshly ground black pepper

Dissolve the yeast in the warm water. Stir in the sugar and set aside.

Mix the remaining ingredients except 1 cup all-purpose flour and the black pepper in a large bowl. Stir with a large spoon or spatula and when the dough is cohesive, turn it out onto a lightly floured surface.

Knead the dough for 10 to 15 minutes or until it is smooth and elastic. Add as much of the reserved flour as necessary to keep the dough from sticking.

Put the dough in a large, lightly oiled bowl, cover with a kitchen towel, and let rise in a warm, draft-free place for about 1 hour or until doubled in volume.

*Coat a baking sheet with nonstick cooking spray.

Using your fist, gently punch down the risen dough. Turn the dough out onto a lightly floured surface and knead for about 1 minute. Shape the dough into a 14-by-6-inch rectangle and lay on the baking sheet. Sprinkle with black pepper. Cover and let rise in a warm, draft-free place for about 45 to 60 minutes or until puffy.

Preheat the oven to 350°F.

Bake the bread for about 35 minutes or until it sounds hollow when tapped. Remove the bread from the pan and let cool on a wire rack.

~~

**To Make in a Bread Machine:** Put all the ingredients except the black pepper in the bread pan in the order listed. (If your machine's manual instructs you to add the ingredients in the reverse order, follow the manual.) Select the basic bread setting and push the start button.

If you prefer to bake the bread in the oven or shape it and bake in the oven, select the dough (or manual) setting. Remove the dough from the machine after it rises once. Follow the instructions beginning at the asterisk (*).

# Corn-Rye-Millet Bread

*This is a solid, sweet, crunchy loaf that provides lots of B vitamins, fiber, and great flavor. Our editor on this book especially liked this one!*

**Yield:** 1 loaf; 18 slices

**Calories per slice:** 159

**Fat per slice:** .66 gram

**Percent of calories from fat:** 4%

1 ¼-ounce package active dry yeast (1 scant tablespoon), at room temperature

1½ cups warm water

½ cup honey

3 cups unbleached all-purpose flour

¾ cup rye flour

¾ cup yellow cornmeal

½ cup millet seeds

1 teaspoon salt

Dissolve the yeast in ½ cup warm water. Stir in 1 tablespoon honey. Set aside.

Mix the remaining ingredients except 1 cup of all-purpose flour in a large bowl. Add the yeast mixture. Stir with a large spoon or spatula and when the dough is cohesive, turn it out onto a lightly floured surface.

Knead the dough for 10 to 15 minutes or until it is smooth and elastic. Add as much of the reserved flour as necessary to keep the dough from sticking.

Put the dough in a large, lightly oiled bowl, cover with a kitchen towel, and let rise in a warm, draft-free place for about 1 hour or until doubled in volume.

*Coat a 9-by-5-inch loaf pan with nonstick cooking spray.

Using your fist, gently punch down the risen dough. Turn the dough out onto a lightly floured surface and knead for about 1 minute. Shape the

(continued)

dough into a loaf and put in the pan. Cover and let rise in a warm, draft-free place for 45 to 60 minutes or until puffy and nearly doubled in volume.

Preheat the oven to 350°F.

Bake the loaf for 40 to 45 minutes or until the bread sounds hollow when tapped. Remove the bread from the pan and let cool on a wire rack.

~.~

**To Make in a Bread Machine:** Put all the ingredients in the bread pan in the order listed. (If your machine's manual instructs you to add the ingredients in the reverse order, follow the manual.) Select the basic bread setting and push the start button.

If you prefer to bake the bread in the oven or shape it and bake in the oven, select the dough (or manual) setting. Remove the dough from the machine after it rises once. Follow the instructions beginning at the asterisk (*).

# Birdseed Bread

Yield: 1 loaf; 18 slices

Calories per slice: 133

Fat per slice: 3.1 grams

Percent of calories from fat: 21%

*The combination of seeds makes this bread healthful and deliciously crunchy. Look for millet seeds (not millet meal) for this bread and expect a subtle, toasty flavor. Take note that the bread rises once and calls only for whole wheat flour—two things that explain the need for a double wallop of yeast for a good rise.*

2 ¼-ounce packages active dry yeast (2 scant tablespoons), at room temperature

1 ½ cups warm water

¼ cup honey

3 ½ cups whole wheat flour

⅓ cup millet seeds

2 tablespoons sunflower seeds

2 tablespoons sesame seeds

2 tablespoons poppy seeds

2 tablespoons vegetable oil

1 teaspoon salt

Dissolve the yeast in the warm water. Stir in the honey. Set aside for about 5 minutes or until bubbly.

Mix the remaining ingredients except 1 cup of flour in a large bowl. Add the yeast mixture. Stir with a large spoon or spatula and when the dough is cohesive, turn it out onto a lightly floured surface.

Knead the dough for 10 to 15 minutes or until it is smooth and elastic. Add as much of the reserved flour as necessary to keep the dough from sticking.

*Coat a 9-by-5-inch loaf pan with nonstick cooking spray.

Shape the dough into a loaf and put in the pan. Cover and let rise in a warm, draft-free place for 45 to 60 minutes or until it rises above the edge of the pan.

Preheat the oven to 350°F.

Bake the loaf for 40 to 45 minutes or until the bread sounds hollow when tapped. Remove the bread from the pan and let cool on a wire rack.

≈≈

**To Make in a Bread Machine:** Put all the ingredients in the bread pan in the order listed. (If your machine's manual instructs you to add the ingredients in the reverse order, follow the manual.) Select the basic bread setting and push the start button.

If you prefer to bake the bread in the oven or shape it and bake in the oven, select the dough (or manual) setting. Remove the dough from the machine after the first kneading. Follow the instructions beginning at the asterisk (*).

T*he whole-grain mustard gives this loaf discernible tang. This is a truly stupendous sandwich bread.*

    2  cups unbleached all-purpose flour
    1½ cups whole wheat flour
    ½  teaspoon salt
    2  tablespoons vegetable oil
    1  tablespoon packed brown sugar
    ⅓  cup whole-grain mustard
    1  ¼-ounce package active dry yeast (1 scant tablespoon), at room
          temperature
    1  cup warm water

# Mustard Seed Bread

Yield: 1 loaf; 18 slices

Calories per slice: 98

Fat per slice: 1.8 grams

Percent of calories from fat: 17%

185

Yeast Breads

Mix all the ingredients except 1 cup of all-purpose flour in a large bowl. Stir with a large spoon or spatula and when the dough is cohesive, turn it out onto a lightly floured surface.

Knead the dough for 10 to 15 minutes or until it is smooth and elastic. Add as much of the reserved flour as necessary to keep the dough from sticking.

Put the dough in a large, lightly oiled bowl, cover with a kitchen towel, and let rise in a warm, draft-free place for about 1 hour or until doubled in volume.

*Coat a 9-by-5-inch loaf pan with nonstick cooking spray.

Using your fist, gently punch down the risen dough. Turn the dough out onto a lightly floured surface and knead for about 1 minute. Shape the dough into a loaf and put in the pan. Cover and let rise in a warm, draft-free place for 45 to 60 minutes or until again doubled in volume.

Preheat the oven to 350°F.

Bake the loaf for 40 to 45 minutes or until the bread is lightly browned and sounds hollow when tapped. Remove the bread from the pan and let cool on a wire rack.

~·~

**To Make in a Bread Machine:** Put all the ingredients in the bread pan in the order listed. (If your machine's manual instructs you to add the ingredients in the reverse order, follow the manual.) Select the basic bread setting and push the start button.

If you prefer to bake the bread in the oven or shape it and bake in the oven, select the dough (or manual) setting. Remove the dough from the machine after it rises once. Follow the instructions beginning at the asterisk (*).

Quick-cooking multigrain cereal is terrific for baking: it's high in fiber and low in fat and sodium, and give breads pleasing texture. We buy it at the local supermarket, but you might also find it at the natural foods store. The most common types are seven- or nine-grain cereals, and there is also four-grain cereal. All are combinations of grains such as rice, wheat, oats, rye, barley, and millet. As you will see from the recipe, you can vary the outcome of the bread by using rye flour instead of whole wheat and by adding molasses rather than honey.

- 2 cups unbleached all-purpose flour
- 1 cup whole wheat or rye flour
- 1 cup quick-cooking multigrain cereal, such as Quaker
- 1 teaspoon salt
- 1/4 cup honey or molasses
- 2 tablespoons vegetable oil
- 1 1/4-ounce package active dry yeast (1 scant tablespoon), at room temperature
- 1 1/4 cups warm water

Mix all the ingredients except 1 cup of all-purpose flour in a large bowl. Stir with a large spoon or spatula and when the dough is cohesive, turn it out onto a lightly floured surface.

Knead the dough for 10 to 15 minutes or until it is smooth and elastic. Add as much of the reserved flour as necessary to keep the dough from sticking.

Put the dough in a large, lightly oiled bowl, cover with a kitchen towel, and let rise in a warm, draft-free place for about 1 hour or until doubled in volume.

*Coat a 9-by-5-inch loaf pan with nonstick cooking spray.

Using your fist, gently punch down the risen dough. Turn the dough out onto a lightly floured surface and knead for about 1 minute. Shape the dough into a loaf and put in the pan. Cover and let rise in a warm, draft-free place for 45 to 60 minutes or until doubled in volume.

Preheat the oven to 350°F.

Bake the loaf for about 40 minutes or until the bread is lightly browned and sounds hollow when tapped. Remove the bread from the pan and let cool on a wire rack.

(continued)

# Multigrain Cereal Bread

<u>Yield:</u> 1 loaf; 18 slices

<u>Calories per slice:</u> 108

<u>Fat per slice:</u> 1.9 grams

<u>Percent of calories from fat:</u> 16%

~~

**To Make in a Bread Machine:** Put all the ingredients in the bread pan in the order listed. (If your machine's manual instructs you to add the ingredients in the reverse order, follow the manual.) Select the basic bread setting and push the start button.

If you prefer to bake the bread in the oven or shape it and bake in the oven, select the dough (or manual) setting. Remove the dough from the machine after it rises once. Follow the instructions beginning at the asterisk (*).

# Roasted Red Pepper Bread

Yield: 1 loaf; 18 slices

Calories per slice: 110

Fat per slice: 1.8 grams

Percent of calories from fat: 15%

*Roasted red pepper puree adds lovely sweet flavor to this savory bread. Serve it with pasta and a green salad, or use it as an appetizer or picnic bread. Making the roasted red pepper puree may take a few extra minutes, but the flavor is unmistakable and always delicious.*

    1 large red bell pepper
    2 tablespoons olive oil
    ½ cup plus 3 to 4 tablespoons warm water, approximately
    1 ¼-ounce package active dry yeast (1 scant tablespoon), at room
        temperature
    2 tablespoons sugar
    2½ cups unbleached all-purpose flour
    1 cup yellow cornmeal
    1 teaspoon dried basil
    1 teaspoon salt

Preheat the broiler.

Broil the red bell pepper about 2 inches from the heat source for 8 to 10 minutes or until the skin turns black. Turn the pepper every few minutes until charred on all sides. Put the charred pepper in a casserole or saucepan, cover, and let sit for about 10 minutes to cool. Using your fingers and a sharp knife, peel away the charred skin. Remove the seeds and ribs from the pepper.

Put the roasted red pepper in a food processor or blender with the olive oil. Puree until smooth. Transfer the puree to a measuring cup and add enough warm water to make ¾ cup of puree. Set aside.

Dissolve the yeast in the remaining ½ cup warm water. Stir in the sugar and set aside for about 5 minutes or until bubbly.

Mix the remaining ingredients except 1 cup of all-purpose flour in a large bowl. Add the red pepper puree and the yeast mixture. Stir with a large spoon or spatula and when the dough is cohesive, turn it out onto a lightly floured surface.

Knead the dough for 10 to 15 minutes or until it is smooth and elastic. Add as much of the reserved cup of flour as necessary to keep the dough from sticking.

Put the dough in a large, lightly oiled bowl, cover with a kitchen towel, and let rise in a warm, draft-free place for about 1 hour or until doubled in volume.

*Coat a baking sheet with nonstick cooking spray.

Using your fist, gently punch down the risen dough. Turn the dough out onto a lightly floured surface and knead for about 1 minute. Divide the dough in half and shape each half into a 16-inch rope. Twist the ropes together into a loaf and carefully put the loaf on the baking sheet. Cover and let rise in a warm, draft-free place for 45 to 60 minutes or until doubled in volume.

Preheat the oven to 350°F.

Bake the loaf for 30 to 35 minutes or until the bread is lightly browned and sounds hollow when tapped. Remove the bread from the pan and let cool on a wire rack.

~~

**To Make in a Bread Machine:** Put all the ingredients in the bread pan in the order listed. (If your machine's manual instructs you to add the ingredients in the reverse order, follow the manual.) Select the basic bread setting and push the start button.

If you prefer to bake the bread in the oven or shape it and bake in the oven, select the dough (or manual) setting. Remove the dough from the machine after it rises once. Follow the instructions beginning at the asterisk (*).

189

Yeast Breads

# Wild Rice–Buttermilk Bread

**Yield:** 1 loaf; 18 slices

**Calories per slice:** 132

**Fat per slice:** 2.1 grams

**Percent of calories from fat:** 14%

**W**e make this wonderful, tender bread over and over again, but have found it unsatisfactory for the bread machine. The machine grinds up the wild rice, robbing the loaf of a slightly crunchy texture. Don't let this discourage you—this is a bread that is so good you won't begrudge it the extra time. Use it for toasting, for sandwiches, or as an accompaniment at suppertime.

1 ¼-ounce package active dry yeast (1 scant tablespoon), at room temperature

¼ cup warm water

¼ cup plus 1 tablespoon molasses

1 cup buttermilk, at room temperature

2 tablespoons vegetable oil

1 teaspoon salt

½ cup yellow cornmeal

½ cup old-fashioned rolled oats

½ cup whole wheat flour

¾ cup cooked and cooled wild rice

2½ cups unbleached all-purpose flour

Dissolve the yeast in the warm water. Stir in 1 tablespoon molasses and set aside for about 5 minutes or until bubbly.

Mix the buttermilk, remaining ¼ cup molasses, oil, and salt in a large bowl. Add the cornmeal, oats, whole wheat flour, and cooked rice. Stir and set aside for 10 minutes.

Add 2 cups all-purpose flour and the yeast mixture to the buttermilk–wild rice mixture. Stir with a large spoon or spatula and when the dough is cohesive, turn it out onto a lightly floured surface.

Knead the dough for 10 to 15 minutes or until it is smooth and elastic. Add as much of the reserved ½ cup flour as necessary to keep the dough from sticking.

Put the dough in a large, lightly oiled bowl, cover with a kitchen towel, and let rise in a warm, draft-free place for about 1 hour or until doubled in volume.

Coat a 9-by-5-inch loaf pan with nonstick cooking spray.

Using your fist, gently punch down the risen dough. Turn the dough out onto a lightly floured surface and knead for about 1 minute. Shape the dough into a loaf and put in the pan. Cover and let rise in a warm, draft-free place for 45 to 60 minutes or until it rises above the edge of the pan.

Preheat the oven to 350°F.

Bake the loaf for 35 to 45 minutes or until the bread sounds hollow when tapped. Remove the bread from the pan and let cool on a wire rack.

**Yeast Breads**

# Potato Bread or Potato Rolls

Yield: 1 loaf; 18 slices or 10 rolls

Calories per slice: 92

Calories per roll: 166

Fat per slice: 1 gram

Fat per roll: 1.7 grams

Percent of calories from fat: 9%

We were thrilled when we first discovered how moist and rich potato yeast breads were. This one is a surefire winner, whether you opt to make a traditional loaf or fashion the dough into fat rolls. If you use leftover mashed potatoes, be sure to omit the salt from the recipe if the potatoes are already salted. Too much salt inhibits the yeast's rising action.

1 medium potato, peeled and cubed (8- to 9-ounce potato)

¾ cup skim milk

1 tablespoon margarine, at room temperature

1 ¼-ounce package active dry yeast (1 scant tablespoon), at room temperature

1 tablespoon sugar

3¼ cups unbleached all-purpose flour

1 teaspoon salt

Put the potato in a saucepan with enough cold water to cover by 1 or 2 inches. Bring to a boil, lower the heat, and simmer for about 15 minutes or until fork tender. Drain the potato, reserving ¼ cup potato water.

Mash the cooked potato with the milk and margarine and set aside.

Dissolve the yeast in the reserved ¼ cup warm potato water. Stir in the sugar and set aside for about 5 minutes or until bubbly.

Mix 2½ cups all-purpose flour, the salt, mashed potatoes, and yeast mixture in a large bowl. Stir with a large spoon or spatula and when the dough is cohesive, turn it out onto a lightly floured surface.

Knead the dough for 10 to 15 minutes or until it is smooth and elastic. Add as much of the reserved flour as necessary to keep the dough from sticking.

Put the dough in a large, lightly oiled bowl, cover with a kitchen towel, and let rise in a warm, draft-free place for about 1 hour or until doubled in volume.

*Coat a 9-by-5-inch loaf pan with nonstick cooking spray.

Using your fist, gently punch down the risen dough. Turn the dough out onto a lightly floured surface and knead for about 1 minute. Shape the dough into a loaf and put in the pan. Cover and let rise in a warm, draft-free place for 45 to 60 minutes or until doubled in volume.

To make rolls, coat a baking sheet with nonstick cooking spray. Divide the dough into 10 pieces and roll each piece into a ball. Set the balls about 1 inch apart on the baking sheet. Cover and let rise in a warm, draft-free place for 45 to 60 minutes or until doubled in volume.

Preheat the oven to 450°F.

Bake the loaf for 45 to 50 minutes and the rolls for 25 to 30 minutes or until the bread is lightly browned and sounds hollow when tapped. Remove the bread from the pan and let cool on a wire rack.

~~

**To Make in a Bread Machine:** Put all the ingredients in the bread pan in the order listed. (If your machine's manual instructs you to add the ingredients in the reverse order, follow the manual.) Select the basic bread setting and push the start button.

If you prefer to bake the bread in the oven or shape it and bake in the oven, select the dough (or manual) setting. Remove the dough from the machine after it rises once. Follow the instructions beginning at the asterisk (*).

# Potato Multigrain Bread

**Yield:** 1 loaf; 18 slices

**Calories per slice:** 123

**Fat per slice:** 1.5 grams

**Percent of calories from fat:** 11%

Leaving the skin on the potato adds extra fiber and vitamins to this bread. If you use red-skinned potatoes, the specks of red look pretty.

1  unpeeled potato, cubed (8- to 9-ounce potato)

1  cup old-fashioned rolled oats

¼  cup 7-grain cereal

1½  cups boiling water

1  ¼-ounce package active dry yeast (1 scant tablespoon), at room temperature

1  teaspoon sugar

2½  cups unbleached all-purpose flour

½  cup whole wheat flour

¼  cup wheat germ

¼  cup honey

1  tablespoon vegetable oil

1  teaspoon salt

Put the potato in a saucepan with enough cold water to cover by 1 or 2 inches. Bring to a boil, lower the heat, and simmer for about 15 minutes or until fork tender. Drain the potato, reserving ¼ cup potato water. Mash the cooked potato and set aside.

Mix the oats and cereal with the boiling water and let sit for 20 to 25 minutes or until lukewarm.

Dissolve the yeast in the reserved ¼ cup warm potato water. Stir in the sugar and set aside for about 5 minutes or until bubbly.

Mix 1½ cups all-purpose flour, the whole wheat flour, wheat germ, honey, oil, salt, oat and cereal mixture, mashed potatoes, and yeast mixture in a large bowl. Stir with a large spoon or spatula and when the dough is cohesive, turn it out onto a lightly floured surface.

Knead the dough for 10 to 15 minutes or until it is smooth and elastic. Add as much of the reserved flour as necessary to keep the dough from sticking.

Put the dough in a large, lightly oiled bowl, cover with a kitchen towel, and let rise in a warm, draft-free place for about 1 hour or until doubled in volume.

*Coat a 9-by-5-inch loaf pan with nonstick cooking spray.

Using your fist, gently punch down the risen dough. Turn the dough out onto a lightly floured surface and knead for about 1 minute. Shape the dough into a loaf and put in the pan. Cover and let rise in a warm, draft-free place for 45 to 60 minutes or until doubled in volume.

Preheat the oven to 350°F.

Bake the loaf for about 40 minutes or until the bread is lightly browned and sounds hollow when tapped. Remove the bread from the pan and let cool on a wire rack.

**To Make in a Bread Machine:** Put all the ingredients in the bread pan in the order listed. (If your machine's manual instructs you to add the ingredients in the reverse order, follow the manual.) Select the basic bread setting and push the start button.

If you prefer to bake the bread in the oven or shape it and bake in the oven, select the dough (or manual) setting. Remove the dough from the machine after it rises once. Follow the instructions beginning at the asterisk (*).

195

Yeast Breads

# Tomato Pull-Apart Bread

**Yield:** 1 large rectangular loaf; 18 servings

**Calories per serving:** 100

**Fat per serving:** 1.8 grams

**Percent of calories from fat:** 16%

**W**e call this pull-apart bread because you are meant to tear the hot loaf into chunks. Chock-full of healthful veggies, it is practically a meal in itself, and rounds out a soup-and-salad dinner very nicely. Our teenagers love to snack on it. For extra flavor, albeit more fat, push chunks of cheddar cheese into the unbaked dough after kneading in the vegetables. While most vegetables can be added raw, carrots should be steamed first for about 3 minutes.

1 ¼-ounce package active dry yeast (1 scant tablespoon), at room temperature

½ cup plus 2 tablespoons warm water

1 tablespoon sugar

½ cup tomato paste

1 large egg white

2 tablespoons vegetable oil

2½ cups unbleached all-purpose flour

¾ cup whole wheat flour

1½ teaspoons Italian seasoning

¾ cup salt

1 tablespoon yellow cornmeal

1 cup chopped raw vegetables, such as red or yellow bell pepper, zucchini, yellow summer squash, red onion, or eggplant

Dissolve the yeast in ½ cup warm water. Stir in the sugar and set aside for about 5 minutes or until bubbly.

Mix the tomato paste with the remaining 2 tablespoons warm water, egg white, and oil. Set aside.

Mix 1½ cups of all-purpose flour, the whole wheat flour, seasoning, and salt. Add the yeast mixture and tomato paste mixture. Stir with a large spoon or spatula and when the dough is cohesive, turn it out onto a lightly floured surface.

Knead the dough for 10 to 15 minutes or until it is smooth and elastic. Add as much of the reserved flour as necessary to keep the dough from sticking.

Put the dough in a large, lightly oiled bowl, cover with a kitchen towel, and let rise in a warm, draft-free place for about 1 hour or until doubled in volume.

*Coat a baking sheet with nonstick cooking spray. Sprinkle the cornmeal over the baking sheet.

Using your fist, gently punch down the risen dough. Turn the dough out onto a lightly floured surface and knead in the raw vegetables. Stretch the dough into an 8-by-12-inch rectangle and carefully put it on the baking sheet. Cover and let rise in a warm, draft-free place for 45 to 60 minutes or until doubled in volume.

Preheat the oven to 350°F.

Bake the loaf for 20 to 25 minutes or until the bread is lightly browned and sounds hollow when tapped. Remove the bread from the pan and serve hot.

~~

**To Make in a Bread Machine:** Make the tomato paste mixture according to the instructions. Put all the ingredients except the cornmeal and vegetables in the bread pan in the order listed. (If your machine's manual instructs you to add the ingredients in the reverse order, follow the manual.) Select the dough (manual) setting and push the start button. Remove the dough from the machine after it rises once. Follow the instructions beginning at the asterisk (*).

# Pumpernickel Raisin Bread

**Yield:** 1 loaf; 18 slices

**Calories per slice:** 118

**Fat per slice:** 1.1 grams

**Percent of calories from fat:** 8%

This is a dense, earthy raisin bread made with rye flour and whole bran cereal for lots of fiber, vitamins, and robust flavor. Rye flour contains no gluten, so we add gluten flour to give a boost to the otherwise heavy dough. Gluten flour is most easily available at natural foods stores. Because our bread machine pulverizes the raisins, we make this by hand. If your machine has a fruit and nut, raisin bread, or sweetbread setting, you might try using it, adding the raisins when the machine indicates you should. However, this is a heavy dough and some machines may labor during kneading.

¾ cup very hot (not boiling) water

¾ cup raisins

1 ¼-ounce package active dry yeast (1 scant tablespoon), at room temperature

1½ cups unbleached all-purpose flour

1¾ cups rye flour

½ cup whole bran cereal

¼ cup gluten flour

1 tablespoon cocoa powder

1 teaspoon salt

½ cup warm water

¼ cup molasses

1 tablespoon vegetable oil

1 tablespoon yellow cornmeal

Pour the hot water over the raisins and let sit for 15 to 20 minutes or until lukewarm. Drain the raisins and reserve the water.

Dissolve the yeast in the reserved, warm raisin water. Set aside for about 5 minutes or until bubbly.

Mix the remaining ingredients except 1 cup of all-purpose flour and the cornmeal in a large bowl. Add the yeast mixture and raisins. Stir with a large spoon or spatula and when the dough is cohesive, turn it out onto a lightly floured surface.

Knead the dough for 10 to 15 minutes or until it is smooth and elastic. Add as much of the reserved flour as necessary to keep the dough from sticking.

Put the dough in a large, lightly oiled bowl, cover with a kitchen towel, and let rise in a warm, draft-free place for about 1 hour or until doubled in volume.

Coat a 9-by-5-inch loaf pan with nonstick cooking spray. Sprinkle the pan with the cornmeal.

Using your fist, gently punch down the risen dough. Turn the dough out onto a lightly floured surface and knead for about 1 minute. Shape the dough into a loaf and put in the pan. Cover and let rise in a warm, draft-free place for 45 to 60 minutes or until doubled in volume.

Preheat the oven to 350°F.

Bake the bread for about 40 minutes or until it sounds hollow when tapped. Remove the bread from the pan and let cool on a wire rack.

# Cinnamon Raisin Bread

**Yield:** 1 loaf; 18 slices

**Calories per slice:** 128

**Fat per slice:** 2 grams

**Percent of calories from fat:** 14%

*Whether you prefer it toasted or plain, cinnamon raisin bread is an all-time classic—and a real Dr. Cookie favorite. Our version is lower in fat and calories than most and so loaded with plump raisins you'll fall in love at first bite.*

1 ¼-ounce package active dry yeast (1 scant tablespoon), at room
   temperature
½ cup warm water
3 tablespoons packed brown sugar
2 cups unbleached all-purpose flour
1½ cups whole wheat flour
1 teaspoon salt
1½ teaspoons ground cinnamon
¾ cup buttermilk, at room temperature
2 tablespoons vegetable oil
1 cup raisins

Dissolve the yeast in the warm water. Stir in the brown sugar and set aside for about 5 minutes or until bubbly.

Mix the remaining ingredients except 1 cup of all-purpose flour in a large bowl. Add the yeast mixture. Stir with a large spoon or spatula and when the dough is cohesive, turn it out onto a lightly floured surface.

Knead the dough for 10 to 15 minutes or until it is smooth and elastic. Add as much of the reserved flour as necessary to keep the dough from sticking.

Put the dough in a large, lightly oiled bowl, cover with a kitchen towel, and let rise in a warm, draft-free place for about 1 hour or until doubled in volume.

*Coat a 9-by-5-inch loaf pan with nonstick cooking spray.

Using your fist, gently punch down the risen dough. Turn the dough out onto a lightly floured surface and knead for about 1 minute. Shape the dough into a loaf and put in the pan. Cover and let rise in a warm, draft-free place for 45 to 60 minutes or until doubled in volume.

Preheat the oven to 350°F.

Bake the loaf for 40 to 45 minutes or until the bread is lightly browned and sounds hollow when tapped. Remove the bread from the pan and let cool on a wire rack.

~·~

**To Make in a Bread Machine:** Put all the ingredients except the raisins in the bread pan in the order listed. (If your machine's manual instructs you to add the ingredients in the reverse order, follow the manual.) Select the basic bread setting and push the start button. Add the raisins during the last 5 minutes of the second kneading. Alternatively, select the fruit and nut (raisin bread, sweet bread) setting and follow the manual's instructions for adding raisins.

If you prefer to bake the bread in the oven or shape it and bake in the oven, select the dough (or manual) setting. Remove the dough from the machine after it rises once. Knead the raisins into the dough. Follow the instructions beginning at the asterisk(*).

# Orange– Cottage Cheese Breakfast Bread

**Yield:** 1 loaf; 18 slices

**Calories per slice:** 85

**Fat per slice:** .4 gram

**Percent of calories from fat:** 4%

**A** light loaf, moistened and subtly flavored with cottage cheese, this bread is wonderful toasted for breakfast. The orange juice concentrate adds vibrant orange flavor, offset deliciously by the golden raisins. And check out the amount of fat. This is practically fat-free!

1 ¼-ounce package active dry yeast (1 scant tablespoon), at room temperature

¼ cup warm water

1 tablespoon honey

2 cups unbleached all-purpose flour

½ cup whole wheat flour

¼ cup orange juice concentrate, at room temperature

1 large egg white, beaten, at room temperature

1 cup low-fat cottage cheese, at warm room temperature

1 teaspoon vanilla extract

½ cup golden raisins

Dissolve the yeast in the warm water. Stir in the honey and set aside for about 5 minutes or until bubbly.

Mix the remaining ingredients except 1 cup of all-purpose flour in a large bowl. Add the yeast mixture. Stir with a large spoon or spatula and when the dough is cohesive, turn it out onto a lightly floured surface.

Knead the dough for 10 to 15 minutes or until it is smooth and elastic. Add as much of the reserved flour as necessary to keep the dough from sticking.

Put the dough in a large, lightly oiled bowl, cover with a kitchen towel, and let rise in a warm, draft-free place for about 1 hour or until doubled in volume.

*Coat a 9-by-5-inch loaf pan with nonstick cooking spray.

Using your fist, gently punch down the risen dough. Turn the dough out onto a lightly floured surface and knead for about 1 minute. Shape the dough into a loaf and put in the pan. Cover and let rise in a warm, draft-free place for 45 to 60 minutes or until doubled in volume.

Preheat the oven to 350°F.

Bake the loaf for 40 to 45 minutes or until the bread is lightly browned and sounds hollow when tapped. Remove the bread from the pan and let cool on a wire rack.

~.~

**To Make in a Bread Machine:** Put all the ingredients except the raisins in the bread pan in the order listed. (If your machine's manual instructs you to add the ingredients in the reverse order, follow the manual.) Select the basic bread setting and push the start button. Add the raisins during the last 5 minutes of the second kneading. Alternatively, select the fruit and nut (raisin bread, sweet bread) setting and follow the manual's instructions for adding raisins.

If you prefer to bake the bread in the oven or shape it and bake in the oven, select the dough (or manual) setting. Remove the dough from the machine after it rises once. Knead the raisins into the dough. Follow the instructions beginning at the asterisk (*).

# Fresh Apple Bread

**Yield:** 1 loaf; 18 slices

**Calories per slice:** 124

**Fat per slice:** .83 gram

**Percent of calories from fat:** 6%

This bread is scrumptious with a cup of hot cider on a chilly autumn afternoon. Or try it toasted and topped with thin slices of cheddar cheese. The bread is so low in fat and calories, the cheese won't propel the snack into fat city.

1 ¼-ounce package active dry yeast (1 scant tablespoon), at room temperature

1 cup warm apple juice

2 cups unbleached all-purpose flour

1 cup old-fashioned rolled oats

1 cup oat bran

1 teaspoon salt

1 teaspoon pumpkin pie spice

1 large egg white, at room temperature

2 tablespoons honey

1 cup grated apple, at room temperature (1 large apple)

Dissolve the yeast in ½ cup warm apple juice. Set aside for about 5 minutes or until bubbly.

Combine the flour, oats, bran, salt, and pie spice in a large bowl.

Beat the egg white with an electric mixer set on medium-high just until foamy. Add the honey, remaining ½ cup apple juice, and grated apple and mix again until blended. Do not overmix.

Add the yeast and about one-third of the dry ingredients to the egg white mixture. Mix well. Add the rest of the dry ingredients a little at a time to make a stiff dough. When the dough is cohesive, turn it out onto a lightly floured surface.

Knead the dough for 10 to 15 minutes or until it is smooth and elastic. Add a little more flour if necessary to keep the dough from sticking.

Put the dough in a large, lightly oiled bowl, cover with a kitchen towel, and let rise in a warm, draft-free place for about 1 hour or until doubled in volume.

*Coat a 9-by-5-inch loaf pan with nonstick cooking spray.

Using your fist, gently punch down the risen dough. Turn the dough out onto a lightly floured surface and knead for about 1 minute. Shape the dough into a loaf and put in the pan. Cover and let rise in a warm, draft-free place for 45 to 60 minutes or until doubled in volume.

Preheat the oven to 350°F.

Bake the loaf for 40 to 45 minutes or until the bread is lightly browned and sounds hollow when tapped. Remove the bread from the pan and let cool on a wire rack.

~~

**To Make in a Bread Machine:** Put all the ingredients in the bread pan in the order listed. (If your machine's manual instructs you to add the ingredients in the reverse order, follow the manual.) Select the basic bread setting and push the start button.

If you prefer to bake the bread in the oven or shape it and bake in the oven, select the dough (or manual) setting. Remove the dough from the machine after it rises once. Follow the instructions beginning at the asterisk (*).

# Apple Rye Bread

**Yield:** 1 loaf; 18 slices

**Calories per slice:** 120

**Fat per slice:** 1.9 grams

**Percent of calories from fat:** 14%

*F*or vegetarian sandwiches, this bread can't be beat. The sweetness of the apples mingles seductively with the rye and caraway—while providing good fiber and many of the health benefits associated with apples. Try it with cold, roasted vegetables or cheese and sliced apples or pears.

1 ¼-ounce package active dry yeast (1 scant tablespoon), at room temperature

1 ¼ cups warm apple juice

2 ½ cups unbleached all-purpose flour

1 cup rye flour

1 tablespoon caraway seeds

1 teaspoon salt

¼ cup molasses

2 tablespoons vegetable oil

½ cup dried apple bits

1 tablespoon yellow cornmeal

Dissolve the yeast in ½ cup warm apple juice. Set aside for about 5 minutes or until bubbly.

Mix the remaining ingredients except 1 cup of all-purpose flour and the cornmeal in a large bowl. Add the yeast mixture. Stir with a large spoon or spatula and when the dough is cohesive, turn it out onto a lightly floured surface.

Knead the dough for 10 to 15 minutes or until it is smooth and elastic. Add as much of the reserved flour as necessary to keep the dough from sticking.

Put the dough in a large, lightly oiled bowl, cover with a kitchen towel, and let rise in a warm, draft-free place for about 1 hour or until doubled in volume.

*Coat a 9-by-5-inch loaf pan with nonstick cooking spray. Sprinkle the pan with the cornmeal.

Using your fist, gently punch down the risen dough. Turn the dough out onto a lightly floured surface and knead for about 1 minute. Shape the dough into a loaf and put in the pan. Cover and let rise in a warm, draft-free place for 45 to 60 minutes or until doubled in volume.

Preheat the oven to 350°F.

Bake the loaf for 35 to 40 minutes or until the bread is lightly browned and sounds hollow when tapped. Remove the bread from the pan and let cool on a wire rack.

~·~

**To Make in a Bread Machine:** Put all the ingredients in the bread pan in the order listed. (If your machine's manual instructs you to add the ingredients in the reverse order, follow the manual.) Select the basic bread setting and push the start button.

If you prefer to bake the bread in the oven or shape it and bake in the oven, select the dough (or manual) setting. Remove the dough from the machine after it rises once. Follow the instructions beginning at the asterisk (*).

# Banana-Date Multigrain Bread

**Yield:** 1 loaf; 18 slices

**Calories per slice:** 145

**Fat per slice:** 1.2 grams

**Percent of calories from fat:** 7%

**W**e combine whole wheat flour, oats, and cornmeal in this healthy bread, tempering the flavor with a cup of ripe bananas, a dose of mellow molasses, and a handful of sweet, sticky dates. Good fiber, good vitamins. Great taste!

1 ¼-ounce package active dry yeast (1 scant tablespoon), at room temperature

⅔ cup warm water

1 tablespoon packed brown sugar

¼ cup molasses

1 cup mashed ripe bananas (about 2 bananas)

2 cups unbleached all-purpose flour

¾ cup whole wheat flour

¾ cup old-fashioned rolled oats

¾ cup yellow cornmeal

1 tablespoon vegetable oil

1 teaspoon salt

½ cup chopped dates

Dissolve the yeast in the warm water. Stir in the brown sugar and set aside for about 5 minutes or until bubbly.

Mix the remaining ingredients except 1 cup of all-purpose flour in a large bowl. Add the yeast mixture. Stir with a large spoon or spatula, and when the dough is cohesive, turn it out onto a lightly floured surface.

Knead the dough for 10 to 15 minutes or until it is smooth and elastic. Add as much of the reserved flour as necessary to keep the dough from sticking.

Put the dough in a large, lightly oiled bowl, cover with a kitchen towel, and let rise in a warm, draft-free place for about 1 hour or until doubled in volume.

*Coat a 9-by-5-inch loaf pan with nonstick cooking spray.

Using your fist, gently punch down the risen dough. Turn the dough out onto a lightly floured surface and knead for about 1 minute. Shape the dough into a loaf and put in the pan. Cover and let rise in a warm, draft-free place for 45 to 60 minutes or until doubled in volume.

Preheat the oven to 350°F.

Bake the loaf for about 40 minutes or until the bread is lightly browned and sounds hollow when tapped. Remove the bread from the pan and let cool on a wire rack.

~~

**To Make in a Bread Machine:** Put all the ingredients in the bread pan in the order listed. (If your machine's manual instructs you to add the ingredients in the reverse order, follow the manual.) Select the basic bread setting and push the start button.

If you prefer to bake the bread in the oven or shape it and bake in the oven, select the dough (or manual) setting. Remove the dough from the machine after it rises once. Follow the instructions beginning at the asterisk (*).

# Banana Oat Bread

**Yield:** 1 loaf; 18 slices

**Calories per slice:** 122

**Fat per slice:** 2 grams

**Percent of calories from fat:** 15%

You've heard it before: bananas for potassium and baked-in moistness; oats for fiber and lower cholesterol. And it's always good advice that's easy to swallow when presented in such a yummy package.

1 cup old-fashioned rolled oats

½ cup boiling water

1 ¼-ounce package active dry yeast (1 scant tablespoon), at room temperature

¼ cup warm water

4 tablespoons packed brown sugar

2 cups unbleached all-purpose flour

1 cup whole wheat flour

1 cup mashed ripe bananas (about 2 bananas)

2 tablespoons vegetable oil

1 teaspoon salt

Stir the oats into the boiling water and let sit for about 10 minutes.

Dissolve the yeast in the warm water. Stir in 1 tablespoon brown sugar and set aside for about 5 minutes or until bubbly.

Mix the remaining ingredients except 1 cup of all-purpose flour in a large bowl. Add the yeast mixture and the oats. Stir with a large spoon or spatula and when the dough is cohesive, turn it out onto a lightly floured surface.

Knead the dough for 10 to 15 minutes or until it is smooth and elastic. Add as much of the reserved flour as necessary to keep the dough from sticking.

Put the dough in a large, lightly oiled bowl, cover with a kitchen towel, and let rise in a warm, draft-free place for about 1 hour or until doubled in volume.

*Coat a 9-by-5-inch loaf pan with nonstick cooking spray.

Using your fist, gently punch down the risen dough. Turn the dough out onto a lightly floured surface and knead for about 1 minute. Shape the dough into a loaf and put in the pan. Cover and let rise in a warm, draft-free place for 45 to 60 minutes or until doubled in volume.

Preheat the oven to 350°F.

Bake the loaf for about 40 minutes or until the bread is lightly browned and sounds hollow when tapped. Remove the bread from the pan and let cool on a wire rack.

～～

**To Make in a Bread Machine:** Put all the ingredients in the bread pan in the order listed. (If your machine's manual instructs you to add the ingredients in the reverse order, follow the manual.) Select the basic bread setting and push the start button.

If you prefer to bake the bread in the oven or shape it and bake in the oven, select the dough (or manual) setting. Remove the dough from the machine after it rises once. Follow the instructions beginning at the asterisk (*).

# Carrot Cake Bread

**Yield:** 1 loaf; 18 slices

**Calories per slice:** 128

**Fat per slice:** 2.2 grams

**Percent of calories from fat:** 15%

*Just what the doctor ordered: a healthy bread that tastes better than carrot cake! This is terrific for B vitamins, beta-carotene, fiber, and all that good stuff. Indulge yourself.*

1 ¼-ounce package active dry yeast (1 scant tablespoon), at room temperature

1 cup warm water

4 tablespoons honey

2 cups unbleached all-purpose flour

1 cup whole wheat flour

⅔ cup old-fashioned rolled oats

⅔ cup oat bran

½ teaspoon ground cinnamon

½ teaspoon grated nutmeg

1 teaspoon salt

2 tablespoons vegetable oil

1½ cups shredded carrots (1 to 2 large carrots)

½ cup raisins

Dissolve the yeast in ½ cup warm water. Stir in 1 tablespoon honey and set aside for about 5 minutes or until bubbly.

Mix the remaining ingredients except 1 cup of all-purpose flour in a large bowl. Add the yeast mixture. Stir with a large spoon or spatula and when the dough is cohesive, turn it out onto a lightly floured surface.

Knead the dough for 10 to 15 minutes or until it is smooth and elastic. Add as much of the reserved flour as necessary to keep the dough from sticking.

Put the dough in a large, lightly oiled bowl, cover with a kitchen towel, and let rise in a warm, draft-free place for about 1 hour or until doubled in volume.

*Coat a 9-by-5-inch loaf pan with nonstick cooking spray.

Using your fist, gently punch down the risen dough. Turn the dough out onto a lightly floured surface and knead for about 1 minute. Shape the dough into a loaf and put in the pan. Cover and let rise in a warm, draft-free place for 45 to 60 minutes or until doubled in volume.

Preheat the oven to 350°F.

Bake the loaf for about 40 minutes or until the bread is lightly browned and sounds hollow when tapped. Remove the bread from the pan and let cool on a wire rack.

~~

**To Make in a Bread Machine:** Put all the ingredients except the carrots and raisins in the bread pan in the order listed. (If your machine's manual instructs you to add the ingredients in the reverse order, follow the manual.) Select the basic bread setting and push the start button. Add the carrots and raisins about 5 minutes before the end of the second kneading. Alternatively, select the fruit and nut (raisin bread, sweet bread) setting and follow the manual's instructions for adding raisins.

If you prefer to bake the bread in the oven or shape it and bake in the oven, select the dough (or manual) setting. Remove the dough from the machine after it rises once. Knead in the carrots and raisins. Follow the instructions beginning at the asterisk (*).

# Thanksgiving Cranberry Oat Rolls

Yield: 10 rolls

Calories per roll: 162

Fat per roll: 4 grams

Percent of calories from fat: 22%

*Cranberries are less expected but twice as welcome in yeast breads as they are in quick breads. These rolls quickly became stars of our Thanksgiving Day table—they'll take center stage on yours, too.*

- 1 cup old-fashioned rolled oats
- 2 tablespoons packed brown sugar
- 1 tablespoon vegetable oil
- 1 teaspoon salt
- 1 cup boiling water
- 1 ¼-ounce package active dry yeast (1 scant tablespoon), at room temperature
- ¼ cup warm water
- 2 tablespoons light molasses
- 1 ½ cups unbleached all-purpose flour
- 1 cup whole wheat flour
- 1 cup fresh or frozen and thawed cranberries
- ¼ cup chopped walnuts

Mix the oats, brown sugar, oil, and salt with the boiling water. Set aside for 15 or 20 minutes or until the oats cool to lukewarm.

Dissolve the yeast in the warm water. Stir in the molasses and set aside for about 5 minutes or until bubbly.

Mix ½ cup all-purpose flour and the whole wheat flour in a large bowl. Add the yeast mixture, oats, cranberries, and walnuts. Stir with a large spoon or spatula and when the dough is cohesive, turn it out onto a lightly floured surface.

Knead the dough for 10 to 15 minutes or until it is smooth and elastic. Add as much of the reserved flour as necessary to keep the dough from sticking.

Put the dough in a large, lightly oiled bowl, cover with a kitchen towel, and let rise in a warm, draft-free place for about 1 hour or until doubled in volume.

*Coat a baking sheet with nonstick cooking spray.

Using your fist, gently punch down the risen dough. Turn the dough out onto a lightly floured surface and knead for about 1 minute. Divide the dough into 10 pieces and shape each one into a roll. Arrange the rolls about 1 inch apart on the baking sheet. Cover and let rise in a warm, draft-free place for 45 to 60 minutes or until doubled in volume.

Preheat the oven to 350°F.

Bake the rolls for 15 to 20 minutes or until they are nicely browned and sound hollow when tapped. Remove the rolls from the pan and let cool on a wire rack.

≈≈

**To Make in a Bread Machine:** Put all the ingredients except the cranberries and walnuts in the bread pan in the order listed. (If your machine's manual instructs you to add the ingredients in the reverse order, follow the manual.) Select the basic bread setting and push the start button. Add the cranberries and walnuts about 5 minutes before the end of the second kneading. Alternatively, select the fruit and nut (raisin bread, sweet bread) setting and follow the manual's instructions for adding raisins.

If you prefer to bake the bread in the oven or shape it and bake in the oven, select the dough (or manual) setting. Remove the dough from the machine after it rises once. Knead in the cranberries and walnuts. Follow the instructions beginning at the asterisk (*).

# Pumpkinseed Bread

**Yield:** 1 loaf; 18 slices

**Calories per slice:** 127

**Fat per slice:** 2.6 grams

**Percent of calories from fat:** 18%

**P**umpkinseeds add interesting flavor and texture to this bread. Use only the seeds you buy in stores—not ones from your Halloween jack-o'-lantern. They won't work.

1 ¼-ounce package active dry yeast (1 scant tablespoon), at room temperature

½ cup warm water

½ cup honey

2½ cups unbleached all-purpose flour

1 cup yellow cornmeal

1½ teaspoons pumpkin pie spice

1 teaspoon salt

2 tablespoons vegetable oil

¾ cup unsweetened pumpkin puree, at warm room temperature

¼ cup pumpkinseeds (unsalted)

Dissolve the yeast in the warm water. Stir in the honey and set aside for about 5 minutes or until bubbly.

Mix the remaining ingredients except 1 cup of all-purpose flour in a large bowl. Add the yeast mixture. Stir with a large spoon or spatula and when the dough is cohesive, turn it out onto a lightly floured surface.

Knead the dough for 10 to 15 minutes or until it is smooth and elastic. Add as much of the reserved flour as necessary to keep the dough from sticking.

Put the dough in a large, lightly oiled bowl, cover with a kitchen towel, and let rise in a warm, draft-free place for about 1 hour or until doubled in volume.

*Coat a 9-by-5-inch loaf pan with nonstick cooking spray.

Using your fist, gently punch down the risen dough. Turn the dough out onto a lightly floured surface and knead for about 1 minute. Shape the dough into a loaf and put in the pan. Cover and let rise in a warm, draft-free place for 45 to 60 minutes or until doubled in volume.

Preheat the oven to 350°F.

Bake the loaf for about 40 minutes or until the bread is lightly browned and sounds hollow when tapped. Remove the bread from the pan and let cool on a wire rack.

~·~

**To Make in a Bread Machine:** Put all the ingredients in the bread pan in the order listed. (If your machine's manual instructs you to add the ingredients in the reverse order, follow the manual.) Select the basic bread setting and push the start button.

If you prefer to bake the bread in the oven or shape it and bake in the oven, select the dough (or manual) setting. Remove the dough from the machine after it rises once. Follow the instructions beginning at the asterisk (*).

For more information or to purchase Dr. Cookie's cookies and other products, call:
    1-800-247-4259
or write:
    Dr. Cookie, Inc.
    18706 North Creek Parkway
    Suite 104
    Bothell, Washington 98011

9

# Index

Agriculture Department, U.S., 8
Almond(s), 12
   -cherry biscotti, 42–43
   macaroons, divine, 40
   peach cream pie, 88
Almost perfect pear bread, 148
*American Family Physician*, 98
Apple:
   cookies, 17
   -cranberry crisp, 102
   gingerbread, hot, 103
   -prune squares, 53
   -raisin compote, hot, 99
   tart, Christine's, 92–93
   yogurt pie, 89
Apple breads:
   double, 145
   fresh, 204–205
   gingerbread with apple, 147
   pie, 146
   rye, 206–207
Apple cakes:
   -bran snack, 62
   carrot-, 68–69
   cranberry-, 64
Applesauce:
   nut cookies, Dr. Cookie's, 18
   oat bran muffins, 117
   oatmeal cookies, 19
Apricot:
   drops, 20
   -pineapple muffins, 127

Banana:
   -carrot cake, 70
   chocolate brownies, 51
   –peanut butter cookies, 32
   surprise cookies, 21
Banana breads:
   chocolate chip–, 157
   multigrain date-, 208–209
   oat, 210–211
   oat bran, 156
   zucchini-oat-, 172
Banana muffins:
   bran-, 118
   oat, 123
   Sunday morning bran-, 119
Berry cobbler, dazzle, 104–105
Berry good cream pie, 86
Beta-carotene, 8
Birdseed bread, 184–185
Biscotti, 42–45
   cherry-almond, 42–43
   orange, 44–45
Biscuits, 116, 140–142
   buttermilk, 140
   multigrain, 141
   potato-dill, 142
"Blind date" bread, 161
Blueberry:
   bread, 149
   cake, 80–81
   muffins, 124

Bran:
  -apple snack cake, 62
  oat, *see* Oat bran
  wheat, *see* Wheat bran
Bran muffins:
  applesauce oat, 117
  banana-, 118
  carrot-, 120
  Dr. Cookie's seed, 122–123
  raisin, 121
  Sunday morning banana-, 119
Breads, *see* Quick breads; Yeast breads
Brownies, 50–52
  chocolate banana, 51
  Dr. Cookie, 50
  fruitcake, 52
Buttermilk, 9
  biscuits, 140
  -wild rice bread, 190–191

Cake flour, 11
Cakes, 59–81
  apple-bran snack, 62
  apple-cranberry, 64
  blueberry, 80–81
  chocolate decadence with raspberry
    sauce, 76–77
  chocolate pudding, 78
  Dr. Cookie's world famous cheesecake, 61
  Marv's favorite fruitcake, 72–73
  oatmeal fresh fruit, 71
  pumpkin squares, 63
  surprise, 74–75
  whole wheat zucchini, 79
  *see also* Carrot cakes
Cancer, 7, 8
Canola oil, 10
Carrot:
  -bran muffins, 120
  cookies, 22
Carrot breads:
  cake, 212–213
  oatmeal-, 162
  zucchini-, 163
Carrot cakes, 66–69
  apple-, 68–69
  banana-, 70
Cereal:
  bread, multigrain, 187–188

Dr. Cookie's granola crust, 85
rice, crisp treats, 57
*see also* Bran; Oat bran; Oatmeal, oat(s);
  Wheat bran
Cheese, 9–10
  cottage, -orange breakfast bread, 202–
    203
  quark, 86
  *see also* Cream cheese frosting
Cheesecake, 60
  Dr. Cookie's world famous, 61
Cherry-almond biscotti, 42–43
Chocolate cakes:
  decadence with raspberry sauce, 76–77
  pudding, 78
Chocolate chip:
  –banana bread, 157
  mint pie, frozen, 93
  muffins, 139
Chocolate chip cookies, Dr. Cookie's, 23
  'n cream frozen pie, 96
Chocolate cookies:
  banana brownies, 51
  cocoa meringues, 39
  date squares, 54
  Dr. Cookie brownies, 50
  heavenly oatmeal, 24
  power-burst, 25
Chocolate pies:
  cream, 90
  frozen fudge pop, 95
Cholesterol, 5, 6–7, 10, 11
Christine's apple tart, 92–93
Cinnamon:
  raisin bread, 200–201
  -raisin whole wheat muffins, 132
Cobbler, dazzle berry, 104–105
Cocoa meringues, 39
Coconut pineapple parfait, 109
*Complete Book of Food Counts, The* (Netzer), 8
Compote, hot apple-raisin, 99
Cookies, 15–57
  apple, 17
  apple-prune squares, 53
  applesauce oatmeal, 19
  apricot drops, 20
  banana surprise, 21
  carrot, 22
  cherry-almond biscotti, 42–43

crisp rice cereal treats, 52
divine almond macaroons, 40
Dr. Cookie's applesauce nut, 18
Dr. Cookie's chocolate chip, 23
fruit 'n spice, 47
gingerbread drops, 26
ginger chews, 46
harvest, 27
hippie, 28
lemon drops, 29
mandelbrot, 49
meringues, 38
orange biscotti, 44–45
orange–poppy seed, 31
prune-oatmeal, 34
pumpkin-date drops, 35
snickerdoodles light, 41
spice puffs, 32
tropical treats, 36
see also Brownies; Chocolate cookies;
    Oatmeal cookies; Peanut butter
    cookies
Corn bread:
    in the round, 164
    rye-millet-, 183–184
    spicy, 165
Cornmeal muffins, 138
Cottage cheese–orange breakfast bread,
    202–203
Cran-apple crisp, 102
Cranberry:
    oat rolls, Thanksgiving, 214–215
    -orange cream, 107
Cranberry bread:
    orange-, 151
    pumpkin-, 152
    raisin-, 150
Cranberry cakes:
    apple-, 64
    date-, 65
Cranberry muffins, 125
    pumpkin-, 126
Cream cheese frosting, 67
    nonfat, 66
Cream pies, 86–88
    berry good, 86
    chocolate, 90
    frozen strawberry, 87
    peach almond, 88

Crisp rice cereal treats, 57
Crisps:
    cran-apple, 102
    plum, 105
Crusts:
    Dr. Cookie's graham cracker, 85
    Dr. Cookie's granola, 85
Curried rice and raisin muffins, 134

Dairy products, 9–10
Date:
    chocolate squares, 54
    -cranberry cake, 65
    -pumpkin drops, 35
Date breads:
    "Blind," 161
    multigrain banana-, 208–209
    no-nut-, 160
Dazzle berry cobbler, 104–105
Diet, planning of, 4
Dill-potato biscuits, 142
Divine almond macaroons, 40
Double apple bread, 145
Dr. Cookie, Inc., 2–3
Dr. Cookie brownies, 50
Dr. Cookie peanut butter squares, 56
Dr. Cookie's applesauce nut cookies, 18
Dr. Cookie's chocolate chip cookies, 23
    'n cream frozen pie, 96
Dr. Cookie's graham cracker crust, 85
Dr. Cookie's granola crust, 85
Dr. Cookie's plum crazy bread, 158
Dr. Cookie's seed bran muffins, 122–123
Dr. Cookie's world famous cheesecake, 61
Dried fruit:
    muffins, 130–131
    potato bread, 154

Eggs, 9
Egg substitutes, 10

Fats, blood, 5, 6–7
Fats, dietary, 4–7
    as ingredients, 10–12
    percentage of calories from, 8
    planning and, 4
    role of, 4–6
    substitutes for, 16
Fiber, dietary, 7–8

Flatbread, herbed, 182–183
Flour, 11
Fresh apple bread, 204–205
Frosting:
    cream cheese, 67
    nonfat cream cheese, 66
Frozen melba, 101
Frozen pies, 93–96
    chocolate chip mint, 93
    Dr. Cookie's cookies 'n cream,
        96
    fudge pop, 95
    peppermint, 94
    strawberry cream, 87
Fruit:
    dried, muffins, 130–131
    dried, potato bread, 155
    yogurt bread, 153
    see also specific fruits
Fruitcake, Marv's favorite, 72–73
Fruitcake brownies, 52
Fruit desserts, 97–113
    cran-apple crisp, 102
    cranberry-orange cream, 107
    dazzle berry cobbler, 104–105
    frozen melba, 101
    hot apple gingerbread, 103
    hot apple-raisin compote, 99
    pared-down pavlova, 108
    peaches 'n cream, 100
    peach melba, 101
    plum crisp, 105
    rice pudding with raisins, 106
    strawberry whip, 112
    trifle, 113
    see also Parfaits
Fruit 'n spice cookies, 47
Fudge pop pie, frozen, 95

Gingerbread:
    with apple, 147
    drops, 26
    hot apple, 103
Ginger chews, 46
Gluten sensitivity, 3
Good morning sunshine bread, 155
Graham cracker crust, Dr. Cookie's,
        85
Granola crust, Dr. Cookie's, 85

Harvest cookies, 27
Heart disease, 6–7
Heavenly chocolate oatmeal cookies, 24
Herb(-ed):
    flatbread, 182–183
    –wheat germ bread, 180–181
High-density lipoprotein (HDL) choles-
        terol, 6, 10
Hiking bread, 166
Hippie cookies, 28
Honey, 5, 12
    -oat bread, 178–179
    and peanut butter breakfast squares, 55
Hot apple gingerbread, 103
Hot apple-raisin compote, 99
Hyperinsulinemia, 5

Ice cream, 9
Ice milk, 9
Ingredients, 8–12
"It depends" philosophy, 3–4

Kidney bean, surprise cake, 74–75
"Know thyself" philosophy, 3

Lactose intolerance, 3, 9
Lava flow, 110
Lemon drops, 29
Litess, 16
Low-density lipoprotein (LDL) cholesterol,
        6–7, 10

Macaroons, divine almond, 40
Mandelbrot, 49
Maple:
    -walnut muffins, 133
    -zucchini bread, 173–174
Margarine, 10, 11
Marv's favorite fruitcake, 72–73
Meringues, 38
    cocoa, 39
    divine almond macaroons, 40
    pared-down pavlova, 108
Milk, 9
    see also Buttermilk
Millet-corn-rye bread, 183–184
Mint:
    chocolate chip pie, frozen, 93
    peppermint pie, frozen, 94

Molasses, 12
Muffins, 115–139
    apricot-pineapple, 127
    banana-oat, 123
    blueberry, 124
    chocolate chip, 139
    cornmeal, 138
    cranberry, 125
    curried rice and raisin, 134
    dried fruit, 130–131
    maple-walnut, 133
    oatmeal-orange, 131
    pineapple, 129
    poppy seed, 135
    pumpkin-cranberry, 126
    pumpkin-pineapple, 128
    sweet potato, 136
    whole wheat cinnamon-raisin, 132
    zucchini, 137
    see also Bran muffins
Multigrain biscuits, 141
Multigrain breads:
    banana-date, 208–209
    cereal, 187–188
    potato, 194–195
Mustard seed bread, 185–186

Netzer, Corinne, 8
Nonfat cream cheese frosting, 66
Nutritive Value of Foods (U.S. Department of
        Agriculture), 8
Nuts, 11–12
    applesauce cookies, Dr. Cookie's, 18
    see also Almond(s); Peanut butter cook-
        ies; Walnut

Oat bran:
    applesauce muffins, 117
    –banana bread, 156
Oatmeal, oat(s):
    banana bread, 210–211
    -banana muffins, 123
    -carrot bread, 162
    cranberry rolls, Thanksgiving, 214–215
    fresh fruit cake, 71
    -honey bread, 178–179
    -orange muffins, 131
    -pumpkin bread, 167–168
    rolled, 11

-zucchini-banana bread, 172
Oatmeal cookies:
    applesauce, 19
    heavenly chocolate, 24
    peanut butter–, 33
    prune-, 34
    raisin-, 30
Oils, 10–11
Olive oil, 10
Orange:
    biscotti, 44–45
    –cottage cheese breakfast bread, 202–
        203
    -cranberry bread, 151
    -cranberry cream, 107
    good morning sunshine bread, 155
    -oatmeal muffins, 131
    –poppy seed cookies, 31

Pacific Southwest Airlines, 2
Pared-down pavlova, 108
Parfaits, 109–111
    lava flow, 110
    pineapple coconut, 109
    rum raisin, 111
Peach(es):
    almond cream pie, 88
    frozen melba, 101
    melba, 101
    'n cream, 100
Peanut butter cookies:
    banana–, 32
    crunchies, 47
    Dr. Cookie squares, 56
    and honey breakfast squares, 55
    oatmeal–, 33
Pear bread, almost perfect, 148
Pepper, roasted red, bread, 188–189
Peppermint pie, frozen, 94
Pfizer Pharmaceutical Company, 16
Pies, 83–96
    apple yogurt, 89
    Dr. Cookie's graham cracker crust for,
        85
    Dr. Cookie's granola crust for, 85
    pumpkin ricotta, 91
    see also Cream pies; Frozen pies
Pineapple:
    coconut parfait, 109

Pineapple (continued)
   muffins, 129
   -zucchini bread, 171
Pineapple muffins, 129
   apricot-, 127
   pumpkin-, 128
Pinto bean, surprise cake, 74–75
Plum:
   crazy bread, Dr. Cookie's, 158
   crisp, 105
Poppy seed:
   muffins, 135
   —orange cookies, 31
Potato:
   bread or rolls, 192–193
   -dill biscuits, 142
   dried fruit bread, 154
   multigrain bread, 194–195
Prune:
   -apple squares, 53
   bread, 159
   -oatmeal cookies, 34
Pudding, rice, with raisins, 106
Pumpernickel raisin bread, 198–199
Pumpkin:
   cake squares, 63
   ricotta pie, 91
Pumpkin bread:
   cranberry-, 152
   oat, 167–168
Pumpkin cookies:
   -date drops, 35
   harvest, 27
Pumpkin muffins:
   cranberry-, 126
   pineapple-, 128
Pumpkinseed bread, 216–217

Quark, 86
Quick breads, 143–174
   almost perfect pear, 148
   apple pie, 146
   banana–oat bran, 156
   "Blind date," 161
   blueberry, 149
   carrot-oatmeal, 162
   carrot-zucchini, 163
   chocolate chip–banana, 157
   corn, in the round, 164

   cranberry-orange, 151
   cranberry-raisin, 150
   date-no-nut, 160
   double apple, 145
   Dr. Cookie's plum crazy, 158
   dried fruit potato, 154
   gingerbread with apple, 147
   good morning sunshine bread, 155
   hiking, 166
   prune, 159
   pumpkin-cranberry, 152
   pumpkin-oat, 167–168
   spicy corn, 165
   wild rice, 168
   yogurt fruit, 153
   yummy yam, 169
   zucchini, 170
   zucchini-maple, 173–174
   zucchini-oat-banana, 172
   zucchini-pineapple, 171

Raisin(s):
   -apple compote, hot, 99
   -oatmeal cookies, 30
   rice pudding with, 106
   rum parfaits, 111
Raisin breads:
   cinnamon, 200–201
   cranberry-, 150
   pumpernickel, 198–199
Raisin muffins:
   bran, 121
   curried rice and, 134
   whole wheat cinnamon-, 132
Raspberry(-ies):
   pared-down pavlova, 108
   sauce, chocolate decadence with, 76–77
Recipes, information about, 88
Rice:
   cereal treats, crisp, 57
   curried, and raisin muffins, 134
   pudding with raisins, 106
   wild, bread, 168
   wild, –buttermilk bread, 190–191
Ricotta pumpkin pie, 91
Roasted red pepper bread, 188–189
Rolls:
   potato, 192–193
   Thanksgiving cranberry oat, 214–215

Rum raisin parfaits, 111
Rye breads:
    apple, 206–207
    corn-millet-, 183–184
    pumpernickel raisin, 198–199

Salt, 3
Serotonin, 5
Snickerdoodles light, 41
Sour cream, peaches 'n, 100
Spice puffs, 37
Spicy corn bread, 165
Strawberry (-ies):
    cream pie, frozen, 87
    lava flow, 110
    trifle, 113
    whip, 112
Sugar, 12
    role of, 4–6
Sunday morning banana-bran muffins, 119
Surprise cake, 74–75
Sweeteners, 4–6, 12
    see also Honey; Sugar
Sweet potato muffins, 136

Tarts:
    Christine's apple, 92–93
    see also Pies
Thanksgiving cranberry oat rolls, 214–215
Tomato pull-apart bread, 196–197
Trifle, 113
Triglycerides, 5, 6, 11
Tropical treats, 36

Vegetable oils, 10–11
Vitamins, 3–4, 7, 8, 9

Walnut:
    applesauce cookies, Dr. Cookie's, 18
    -maple muffins, 133
Wheat bran:
    –banana muffins, 118
    –banana muffins, Sunday morning, 119
    –carrot muffins, 120
    raisin muffins, 121
    seed muffins, Dr. Cookie's 122–123
Wheat germ–herb bread, 180–181
Whole wheat:
    bread, 177–178

cinnamon-raisin muffins, 132
    zucchini cake, 79
Wild rice:
    bread, 168
    –buttermilk bread, 190–191
Wurtman, Judith, 5

Yam bread, yummy, 169
Yarnall, Gail, 2
Yeast breads, 175–217
    apple rye, 206–207
    banana-date multigrain, 208–209
    banana oat, 210–211
    birdseed, 184–185
    carrot cake, 212–213
    cinnamon raisin, 200–201
    corn-rye-millet, 183, 184
    fresh apple, 204–205
    herbed flatbread, 182–183
    honey-oat, 178–179
    multigrain cereal, 187–188
    mustard seed, 185–186
    orange–cottage cheese breakfast, 202–203
    potato, 192–193
    potato multigrain, 194–195
    pumpkinseed, 216–217
    roasted red pepper, 188–189
    Thanksgiving cranberry oat rolls, 214–215
    tomato pull-apart, 196–197
    wheat germ–herb, 180–181
    whole wheat, 177–178
    wild rice–buttermilk, 190–191
Yogurt, 9
    apple pie, 89
    frozen, 9
    fruit bread, 153
    peaches 'n cream; 100
Yummy yam bread, 169

Zucchini:
    muffins, 137
    whole wheat cake, 79
Zucchini bread(s), 170
    carrot-, 163
    maple-, 173–174
    oat-banana-, 172
    pineapple-, 171